READING BETWEEN THE LINES
Teachers and Their Racial/Ethnic Cultures

Mary E. Dilworth

With a Foreword by Linda Darling-Hammond

Published by

**CLEARINGHOUSE
ON TEACHER
EDUCATION**

ERIC Clearinghouse on Teacher Education
and
American Association of Colleges for Teacher Education
One Dupont Circle, Suite 610
Washington, DC 20036-2412

August 1990

CITE AS:
Dilworth, Mary E. (1990). *Reading Between the Lines: Teachers and Their Racial/Ethnic Cultures*. (Teacher Education Monograph: No. 11). Washington, D.C.: ERIC Clearinghouse on Teacher Education and American Association of Colleges for Teacher Education.

MANUSCRIPTS:
The ERIC Clearinghouse on Teacher Education invites individuals to submit proposals for writing monographs for the Teacher Education Monograph Series. Proposals should include:
1. a detailed manuscript proposal of not more than five pages;
2. a vita; and
3. a writing sample.

PREPAID ORDERS:
ERIC CLEARINGHOUSE ON TEACHER EDUCATION
One Dupont Circle, NW, Suite 610
Washington, DC 20036-2412
(202) 293-2450

Single copy—$20 (fourth-class postage included)

Library of Congress Catalog Card Number: 90-083152

ISBN: 0-89333-068-X

Office of Educational Research and Improvement
U.S. Department of Education

This publication was prepared with funding from the Office of Educational Research and Improvement, U.S. Department of Education under contract number RI88062015. The opinions expressed in this report do not necessarily reflect the positions or policies of OERI or DOE.

Contents

Tables

Foreword

Reading Between the Lines is a much needed consciousness-raising document. It identifies important questions for researchers and teacher educators about the ways in which race, ethnicity and culture influence teachers' motivations and intentions for teaching, as well as their expectations of their students and of their own professional lives.

As the monograph rightly observes, these are matters that have been too rarely addressed by research and—though they matter greatly for student success as well as for teacher recruitment and preparation—have been largely unacknowledged by teacher education programs. In pointing out the gaps in our knowledge, Mary Dilworth constructs an agenda for future research while framing the considerations that should guide this research. These include a heightened sensitivity to the reality of different experiences and truths for members of racial and ethnic minority groups in the United States, a willingness to explore openly diversity in teachers' views and motivations rather than to assume either uniformity on the one hand or stereotypic differences on the other, and a capacity to integrate research on teaching with research on the cultures of teachers and learners.

Not all of the burden rests on researchers, however. Teacher educators can begin to incorporate knowledge made available in other parts of the academy into the preparation of teachers as well. As James Comer notes: "Preservice programs—in and outside the discipline of education—should provide all students with an understanding of how structural forces, policies, and practices impact communities, groups and families, and child development."

Given the growing diversity of students in public schools, the mission of conveying these understandings must extend to all prospective teachers in all teacher preparing institutions. At the same time, policymakers and educators at all levels must tackle the array of forces, so well documented here, that contribute to an acute and growing shortage of minority teachers. As this report aptly observes: "Given the persistent national concern for a competitive edge in the world economy, for social order and the demographic realities of this country, it is naive to perceive a quality education for any child that is developed by a parochial educational system and delivered by a homogeneous teaching force."

The question is not which of these strategies to pursue but how best to mobilize the educational community and the broader society in pursuit of both a culturally informed *and* a culturally diverse teaching population. This report provides an important first step in that process. In its wide-ranging treatment of racial and cultural realities and issues in America, it provides a map of the terrain that committed educators must travel en route to a deeper understanding of the interactions between culture and teaching. In Socratic manner, the report does not provide easy answers; rather it poses the questions that are the necessary starting points for our diverse personal and professional odysseys. For it is in acknowledging this diversity that our profession can become both whole and more wholly connected to the students it serves.

LINDA DARLING-HAMMOND
TEACHERS COLLEGE,
COLUMBIA UNIVERSITY

Acknowledgments

M any individuals contributed to the development of this mono-graph. David Imig (American Association of Colleges for Teacher Education) provided substantial feedback on earlier versions of this piece. Linda Darling-Hammond (Columbia University, Teachers College), Antoine Garibaldi (Xavier University, LA), Robert Kottkamp (Hofstra University) and Sharon Nelson Barber (Stanford University) offered very useful critiques of the subsequent draft.

AACTE and ERIC Clearinghouse staff Dorothy Stewart, Mark Lewis, Deborah Rybicki and Cathleen Siegel, were particularly helpful in securing research material and providing other technical assistance. Last but not least, Audrey Vaughan and Clearinghouse associate director Judy Beck provided expert editorial guidance.

My thanks to all.

MARY E. DILWORTH

Introduction

I t is a matter of quality and it is a matter of equality. As the nation's school population becomes more diverse, the teaching force becomes increasingly homogeneous. The implications of this disturbing trend go well beyond the lack of valuable role models for children of color and have a direct relationship to the quality of education for all students.

Given their culturally diverse backgrounds, and academic training defined by the White majority, Black, Hispanic and other minority teachers possess a consummate understanding of the relationship between education and this society. This knowledge enhances the quality of education when these teachers offer their students broader and more complex interpretations of the educational curriculum, and when they translate and interpret for their majority peers, in educational terms, the cultural backgrounds of their students. Yet, Black, Hispanic, Asian and Native American teachers are few and far between.

Gradually, the education community has come to recognize the value of minority teachers and has initiated some activities to encourage their participation in the profession. However, the few programs and policies designed to recruit a larger pool of these teachers are limited in scope, isolated in placement and, for the most part, have not had a significant impact. While recognizing that teachers of color provide desirable diversity in the classroom, recruitment program administrators fail to recognize that their backgrounds, and resultant needs and motivations, also vary.

Even the most optimistic educators concede that the best recruitment efforts will not meet the immediate need for more Black, Hispanic and other minority teachers. Consequently, those in research and development are urged to devise training models that will inform all prospective teachers how best to educate racially and culturally diverse students. Unfortunately, it appears that the educational community is unprepared to meet this challenge. The results—minority children typically make fewer academic gains than their White cohorts. While there is significant research

xi

on the precepts of good educational practice, very little joins this information with knowledge on the backgrounds and cultures of the recipients.

The data do provide some justification for pursuing this line of inquiry. For instance, there is a body of literature that clearly indicates that a teacher's background does influence the expectations that she or he holds for students of various racial/ethnic cultures and that such expectations subsequently influence the achievement of these students (Jordan Irvine, 1990). In addition, there is evidence that minority students, more so than others, are often lost in the transition between the culture of home and the culture of school and that culturally informed teachers can play a significant role in easing this adjustment (Delpit, 1986; Eisenhart, 1989).

Although there are apparent racial/ethnic group differences in custom, family structure, language, religion, and often cited variations in socioeconomic background, some may argue that race and ethnicity have very little to do with the way teachers approach and conduct their work. Since the research literature is so limited in this area it is difficult to accept or deny this premise. If, as it appears, minority teachers contribute substantially to the quality of learning, it is essential that this line of inquiry be pursued. This work is offered as a starting point for this discussion.

Reading Between the Lines may be useful in two ways. First, by describing background, motivational and experiential differences, as well as reward and incentive preferences between and among teachers of various racial/ethnic groups, current and future recruitment efforts can be better targeted and become more effective. Second, by presenting an overview of the research literature and identifying gaps relative to racial and ethnic culture, those in research and development may be encouraged to close these gaps and assist in developing teaching models that embrace this diversity in a better way.

In order to meet these two objectives a number of questions were raised. For example, gaps in the literature present a significant challenge to this work. Should the discussion be restricted to the little that is known about teachers' racial/ethnic backgrounds and cultures, or should this information be couched among somewhat educationally remote factors that provide a better understanding of teaching and racial and ethnic cultures generally? The decision to review topics such as the socioeconomic conditions of minority groups in this country seemed to be a necessary and desirable component in the discussion. If teaching is to embrace the diversity of its ranks and its students, then it seems only natural that a general understanding of this diversity as it arrives in the school or in the academy should be a first step.

Another question of concern—i.e., Should student diversity and attitudes be addressed, or should the discussion be limited to teachers' diversity and attitudes?—was cause for deliberation. Although there is much more to be examined, there are generally more race-specific data available on students' performance and attitudes than on teachers'. In probing the cultural backgrounds of Black, Hispanic, Asian and Native American teachers, we simultaneously understand a bit more about students from these same groups. In essence, this manuscript attempts to shed new light on some issues familiar to us, and expose those factors somewhat foreign to us with new and greater understandings as a goal.

Content Overview

This monograph is organized in five chapters. Chapter I, "The Culture of Teachers: The Culture of Teaching," offers a general overview of common knowledge regarding the nature or culture of the profession and its participants; the generally accepted notions regarding teaching as an occupation; and the attitudes or needs that may prompt an individual to pursue this occupation. Although the research literature is generous in its review and analysis of teachers as an occupational group, very little contributes to thinking on subgroups of this population and how they may differ from others in their attraction to and conduct of teaching. Chapter II, "Studying Teachers' Racial/Ethnic Cultures," suggests that for various reasons, educational researchers have generally overlooked this line of inquiry, which holds promise for recruiting and retaining teachers of color, as well as for explaining their performance and the achievement of children from these groups. Chapter III, "The Teaching Population: Present and Future," provides a general description of the current and prospective teaching population and leads into Chapter IV, a discussion of racial and ethnic differences in teacher "Motivation, Rewards and Incentives." Last, Chapter V, "Racial/Ethnic Cultures," provides a brief descriptive profile of the major minority groups in this country and is a reference for much of the discussion.

Limitations

A true comparison of teachers by race and ethnicity deserves a volume that thoroughly probes various anthropological, historical and sociological interpretations of education as they relate to all races, many cultures, and certainly beyond the borders of the United States. For example, there are several approaches to the anthropology of education: the process of cultural transmission of how children learn the official curriculum; or the approach that focuses on the function of schooling as a means for reproducing the social order (Anderson-Levitt, 1987). While the latter is an underlying assumption, and possibly the purpose of this discussion, this monograph will not probe in or around this issue.

Unfortunately, the paucity of relevant data for even the major racial/ethnic groups often limits a discussion to the two most predominant in this country, Black and Hispanic Americans. Literature regarding Asian and Native Americans is provided when available. As Jiobu (1988) notes "... empirical voids still exist, especially when studying groups other than Blacks. Data are sporadic, inconsistent in format and source, and limited in scope" (p. ix).

This presentation is limited further since these groups should be additionally classified by country of ancestral origin, e.g., Mexico, Japan, West and East Indies, etc. The absence of data makes this an unrealistic goal. Consequently, it appears that some discussion referencing broad racial/ethnic categories may be more important than no discussion at all.

Finally, semantics present a problem. For instance, at present there is an effort within the Black community to adopt the term "African American" to reflect ancestral origin. In addition, the term "minority" also seems limiting and inappropriate when describing individuals from groups that collectively dominate, in number, many of the nations' cities and institutions. Since the relationships and correlations suggested throughout this work may be unfamiliar, new and possibly confusing to the reader, this discussion will not force new vocabulary.

I

The Culture of Teachers: The Culture of Teaching

There is a simplicity of spirit in the literature that describes teachers. There is a general consensus within the academic community on what type of individual enters the profession and there is a naive understanding of what type of rewards can be and are drawn from an individual's participation in it. Although the cultural backgrounds that teachers bring to their work are inextricably tied to performance, the literature in this regard focuses almost exclusively on basic demographic data and pales by comparison to treatment of other issues.

Recent research suggests that the conventional wisdom regarding the nature of teachers must and should be examined once again, particularly in light of the new socioeconomic order that has tested minorities' and women's commitment to the profession and forced a greater level of participation in the work force (Feiman-Nemser & Floden, 1986; Joseph & Green, 1986; Darling-Hammond, Johnson, Pittman, & Ottinger, 1987). Most important, this re-examination must probe beyond the typical factors of gender and experience and take into account the cultural backgrounds of teachers. As Mills and Buckley (1989) note, culture provides the rules by which educators consciously and unconsciously operate as they design and deliver instruction, set role expectations for self and students, assign value to the worth of students' contributions and interpret the behavior of students. The following provides an overview of the conventional wisdom on the nature of the profession, teachers and their motivations.

The Nature of the Profession

One would assume that changes in the nation's social and economic character would have influenced the role and even the type of individual choosing teaching as a career. However, this is not the case. The information drawn regarding their backgrounds and attitudes has remained fairly constant over time. As was the case 40 years ago, the teaching force is primarily supported by White females from somewhat higher socioeco-

1

nomic backgrounds than their male counterparts. And as in the past, these women pursue this line of work to "help children grow and develop" (Rury, 1989).

The profession also remains in an unseemingly steady state. Warren (1989), pointing directly to persistent economic, political and cultural conditions, states, "Although teachers' working conditions have improved dramatically over the past two decades, we detect recurring conflicts and problems that have required attention in each generation rather than inexorable movement toward the ideal state" (p. 3).

One factor that appears to contribute to the somewhat monotonous tale that is told of teachers is the service nature of the work and accompanying prestige (or lack thereof). According to Charters (1963), teachers, as do others, garner an extrinsic value from their occupation. The value, measured in the honor, deference or prestige accorded the occupation, is derived from the culture at large and generally applies to the incumbent regardless of his/her capacity to do the work.

In this country, service work is expected, bought and paid for, but it is not necessarily valued. Morals are respected but are not rewarded in any special way by the public. If teaching "is a valuable service of special moral worth" as Lortie's (1975) "Five Towns" subjects suggest, the value quickly reaches the point of diminishing returns. It fosters the notion that the profession is always responsive and always good. This pious perception may be further fueled by the dominance of women in the profession. As researchers such as Dreeben (1970) contend, "Occupations open to women appeal more to the heart than to the mind."

If teaching is service work then teachers, for the most part, are public servants. Possibly in response to this general public sentiment, they individually and collectively have been fairly docile in constructing and manipulating the content and process of their trade in any way other than those traditionally and duly appointed to labor. "Empowerment," as defined by Maeroff (1988), could change some of this. He holds that teachers "are undervalued by themselves and others and are not likely to feel they have much power. . . . Those who see themselves as having less worth than others are not likely to feel a sense of authority about what they do" (p. 19). Maeroff's statement implies that to attain professional status, within the public sector framework, there should or must be a solution, but not necessarily monetary, wherein individuals can experience a greater level of integrity.

Lortie (1975) suggests that the service nature of the profession is a recruitment tool, attracting individuals who for the most part approve of prevailing practice more than they are critical of it. At the same time, the good nature of the profession may drive aggressive and broad-minded individuals away from teaching with equal force. In a similar vein, Haggstrom, Grissmer and Darling-Hammond (1988) note that attraction to

2

teaching is also motivated by supply and demand conditions. They offer that a high demand for new teachers "... encourages individuals at the margin to enter the profession who have less 'taste' or commitment for teaching" (p. 16).

If, as is commonly held, the prestige accorded teaching determines the kind of person attracted to the profession, then the public expectations of teacher performance, and of student learning and outcomes, must be minimal. Clifford (1989) provides that the cultural stereotype of the teacher reflects the public's "expression of hopes and fears, prejudice, wishful thinking, the desire to appear large-minded while protecting one's narrowest interests" (p. 311). In addition, and possibly more important, the low prestige of the profession has an impact on the perceptions and performance of its group in several ways: levels motivation to fulfill classroom functions; discourages independence of thought and freedom of action; suggests a lack of influence or authority in the teaching/learning process; and diverts energy from occupational functions toward activities designed to enhance their economic sustenance (Charters, 1963).

Problems associated with the low prestige of the profession have also been associated with the low esteem that minority groups in this society experience. Gramb (1949) explains this when he states that teachers are inclined to reject their membership group—to disqualify themselves with their occupation—a matter made more difficult ... by the "conspicuousness" of their status. On the other hand, since teaching was and is one of the few professions relatively accessible to groups typically denied entry in other fields, the participation of Blacks and other immigrant groups undermined the social status of the profession in the early years of the century (Rury, 1989). As will be discussed in Chapter IV, there are differences between and among members of racial and ethnic groups in the values and perceptions that they hold for their work. However, it is possible that these factors are of less influence on their work attitudes than are their perceptions of the occupation as a whole.

Prestige or social status, for almost any field, relies heavily on income level. The teaching profession is no exception. Teachers' income has been compared to others for nearly a century. Sedlak and Schlossman (1987), in a historical review of the nature of teaching as an occupation, conclude that teaching, as any occupation, has been shaped significantly by economic incentives. Salaries for teachers, as in other professions, have been subject to a number of external influences, e.g., supply/demand, economic inflation and depressions. However, Sedlak and Schlossman offer the general conclusion that teaching salaries have increased steadily in absolute terms throughout the century. Further, they state that comparing teacher salaries is a tool of sociologists in analyzing status, and that educators seeking to improve salaries have long highlighted the earnings advantages of other workers.

3

It is also interesting to note that during the period when teachers were not required to attend and complete four years of college, comparisons were often made with "high-grade" clerical and other skilled laborers. Charters (1963), in reporting comparative data from the 1950s, found teachers' salaries roughly comparable to the earnings of those working in manufacturing but substantially below the incomes of physicians, lawyers and dentists. Over three decades later, Darling-Hammond et al. (1987) report that teachers' salaries are slightly higher than clerical workers, are on par with sales and lower-level health workers, and are still significantly below salaries of engineers, accountants, lawyers, salaried and self-employed physicians.

Once a bachelor's degree became the minimum requirement and expectation, comparisons with physicians and lawyers became more frequent. Seldom do such comparisons focus on the supply and demand inequities between teaching and these other occupations. One reason for not pursuing comparisons along these lines may be the reality that the economy cannot support the profession at a similar rate (Dilworth, 1984).

Casey and Apple (1989), in a critical review of Lortie and Dreeben, suggest that research comparing teaching career paths with occupations that exemplify male career paths such as law, engineering, business and the military are inappropriate. When such comparisons are made, teachers consistently are found wanting in terms of prestige and its prerequisites—esoteric expertise and autonomy. They further suggest that this "gender deficit" theory of teaching does not provide an understanding of the way gender, and its accompanying resistances and contradictions, work their way in and out of teachers' lives. The same thinking has applicability to race and ethnicity.

The unionization of teaching (1940s and 1950s), although instrumental in the improved conditions and salaries of its constituents, also prompted an intellectual debate on whether teachers should be viewed as professionals or as workers. Teachers, theoretically, may be placed in "contradictory class locations" simultaneously "sharing the interests of both petty bourgeoisie and the working class." Casey and Apple (1989) hold that this dual position, particularly during times of fiscal crisis and labor disputes, contributes to the deprofessionalism of teaching (p. 178).

As Charter notes, "income level may be closely correlated with social standing in the United States, but it is not perfectly correlated with social standing, as the cases of artist, minister, bartender, and school teacher attest" (p. 745). As he and Maeroff (1988) provide, there are other bases of evaluation for teaching. "Assumptions have been made as to what social statuses are likely to produce the best teachers; however, these assumptions have been little more than the embodiment of popular conceptions or stereotypes" (p. 723).

4

The academic community's concept of a good teacher has significantly changed since Charter's comments in the 1960s. However, the question remains whether or not recruitment, selection, training, hiring and retention practices have kept pace with these new aspirations. The research and reform literature of the 1980s [e.g., Berliner (1986), Darling-Hammond and Green (1988), Holmes Group (1986), Shulman (1987)] suggests that the next generation of teachers should have a firm grasp on the content of the subjects they teach; the capability to apply this knowledge in a classroom setting; the skills to devise appropriate learning tools; the ability to make informed assessments of students' work; and the inclination to analyze their own work as well as the work of others in the school environment. Further, there is a demographic imperative that these new teachers will be culturally diverse, as well as culturally aware in order to educate effectively students of varying backrounds.

Although teacher education has begun to institute courses and experiences that address these criteria, little suggests that these will be the standards used by administrators when employment decisions are made. As Wise, Darling-Hammond and Berry (1987) note, "Teacher selection is a process embedded in a social-political-organizational context. As practiced today, it is the result of both careful planning, historical accident, and political compromise" (p. 79).

Certainly, answers to the far reaching questions, "Is teaching for the 'successful' or the 'unsuccessful' members of society? Is it populated by the intellectuals and scholars of the society, by members of the working class, by members of agrarian derivation, by civil servant class, or members of the business community?" (Charters, 1963), would present challenges to the current system that policymakers would like to avoid. For instance, if it is concluded that public school teachers are not the intellectuals and scholars of society, what viable means, given supply, demand and economic realities, does the public have to change the situation? On what grounds would it be done?

The Nature of the Professional

If service work, such as teaching, represents goodness, then the woman's role in staffing the public schools is consistent. Gender is one of the fundamental organizing principles in society—as important a category for analysis as class or race or age. "Passivity, lack of divergent thinking, absence of intellectual rigor, conformity, compliance, and narrow focus are common descriptors of traditional schools and traditional women" (Acker, 1989, p. 1). As Lubeck (1988) states, "different ways of thinking and behaving become differentially rewarded in society at large, and membership in particular racial, ethnic, class, and gender groups has

5

traditionally entailed the ascription of particular roles and statuses within a broader system of relations" (p. 55).

The fact that the profession is dominated by women has obvious and far-reaching implications for the narrow and limited attention devoted to its description. Although there are some (Clifford, 1989) who provide contrary arguments, as Freidus (1989) notes, there is a "gender oriented hierarchy that dominates public school education that has existed for more than a century." Lortie (1975) devotes significant attention to this reality, suggesting that the time compatability, so necessary for a woman's participation in the work force, is a direct benefit and keeps the teaching force functional. Female dominance in the ranks of the profession has also been identified as contributing to the maintenance of a status quo in the structure of schooling and the nature of the profession. Authors such as Cunnison (1989) and Orum (1989) suggest that the status quo may be rooted in a sexist perception that men have little to gain in disrupting.

The primary motivation for entering the profession is something that has remained constant. The notion that teachers are caring, loving individuals who are drawn to the profession because they wish to help young people grow and develop, and who garner mostly intrinsic rewards (e.g., student achievement) as a result, has been tested and retested and yet withstood decades of educational innovation, maturity and transition. Although some (Feiman-Nemser & Floden, 1986; Tyack, 1967), hold that this sentiment was consciously imposed and fostered more than a century ago to accommodate the economic and social conditions of the time, it is a sentiment that nevertheless was successfully propagated, adopted and internalized by the American citizenry and more importantly was embraced by those who fill the ranks of the profession.

The most recent surveys of teacher education students indicate that very little has changed over time. Students of nearly four decades ago offer virtually the same responses to the motivation question (Wilcox & Beigel, 1953; AACTE, 1990). This suggests at least two things: the professionals in teaching are more homogeneous than those in other disciplines; and/or the same question is being asked in similar fashion and focus—time and time again. It has been suggested that prospective teachers' consistent responses in terms of motivation possibly are learned responses, and that motivation is being gauged by traditional instruments that are possibly inaccurate (Joseph & Green, 1986; Lortie, 1975). However, this probability has not deterred researchers from probing motivation over and over again.

According to Acker (1989), there are several dimensions to examining career (profession). There is the individual experience wherein knowledge regarding aims, ambitions and feelings is sought; the structural perspective that recognizes the social and economical environment that accommodates the career; and there are the rules or conventions that control career movement. She holds that research has failed to integrate these three areas, fostering a dichotomous presentation. On one end of the spectrum, teachers are considered rational individuals organizing their career path; at the other end teachers are mere victims of the system, unable to exercise any freedom of choice.

By studying teachers' cultural backgrounds one is forced to recognize these three areas as this nation tends to offer separate and distinct social, economic and career mobility options for individuals of different racial/ ethnic groups. As the following discussion explains, this approach requires a different type of thinking and analysis than has been employed by most educational researchers.

II

Studying Teachers' Racial/Ethnic Cultures

A discussion of both real and perceived differences between and among U.S. teachers of different racial/ethnic membership must be predicated on some understanding and discussion of the basic ethos of those cultures. Previous surveys and studies of teachers occasionally, but more frequently in recent years, allowed for racially/ethnically mixed samples or situations. Yet, the results are treated and analyzed on generic White, Anglo-Saxon, Protestant principles, judgments and understandings. To gleen real and contemporary inferences from current educational research literature on teaching, one must read between the lines.

This chapter focuses on researchers' perceptions of culture within education; the methods employed in such research; and factors necessary when examining the racial and ethnic dimensions of culture. It is important that educators be aware of their own attitudes, behaviors, situations and expressions that reinforce prejudicial beliefs (Pang, 1988), and this can only be accomplished through familiarity with the various racial/ethnic cultures. Such examination need not be devisive, but will necessarily contribute to a deeper understanding of teaching and learning as it relates to many rather than to a single group.

Perceptions of Culture

Culture, regarding teachers, is typically defined introspectively from within schools, with certain faint recognition of external forces. Culture, in the educational literature, typically relates to the school and its environment and its actors (i.e., principals, students, parents and peers) coupled with legitimate attention to gender (Feiman-Nemser & Floden, 1986; Nigris, 1988; Ortiz & Mitchell, 1987). It is a rare occasion when analysis branches beyond these dimensions to consider "the messy, noisy world" (Lightfoot, 1987) or the racial/ethnic background of its staff (Kottkamp, Cohen, McClosky & Provenzo, 1987).

In citing O'Brien (1984), McCarthy and Apple (1988) note that "both mainstream and radical educational researchers have tended to undertheorize and marginalize or 'common'ize phenomena associated with race and gender. We therefore know less than we should about the specific content of racial or sexual oppression in schooling." In addition, they contend, ". . . less conceptual energy has been spent on understanding the relationship between schools and the persistence and reproduction of social and economic disadvantages that systematically affect minority youth and women" than has been devoted to White working-class males (p. 9).

"The question, whether even a majority of teachers share a common culture, has not been answered" (Feiman-Nemser & Floden, 1986). One possible reason for what Lortie terms this "odd gap" in salient points regarding teachers' subjective world may be the labor requirements of the profession. Teachers are not expendable commodities, and the selection of individuals on subjective grounds would be indefensible. No other occupations visibly screen their rank on such grounds.

Regarding culture, Lortie (1975), in his classic sociological depiction of teachers and their nature, provides that there are certain "themes" that likely apply to any or all teachers: interpersonal, service, continuation, material and time compatability. Each contributes to some extent to the decision (primarily of women) to enter teaching. Without countering this view, others have suggested that there may be more factors in the decision to enter and stay in the profession. For instance, Feiman-Nemser and Floden (1986) provide greater allowance for what teachers bring and pick up as they teach, by examining the "culture" of the school experience, the influence of peers, superiors, parents and students.

Although these authors do not focus on the racial/ethnic dimension of culture, they do suggest areas of difficulty that are useful in such analyses. Specifically, they provide that studying cultures implies inferences about knowledge, values and norms for action, none of which can be directly observed; that the existence of many teaching cultures poses additional questions, e.g., which culture or cultures to study, how differences between and similarities within cultures can be documented; how researchers must neither evaluate a culture by inappropriate, external standards nor fall into the realistic trap of asserting that every culture is good.

Feiman-Nemser and Floden (1986) also inadvertently offer some justification for studying culture within a racial/ethnic context. By exploring ". . . how teachers define their own work . . . one can also form predictions about how teachers are likely to respond to policy initiatives and guide efforts to shape them. As the nation requests and SCDEs seek to provide for a different generation of teachers, this will become of maximum importance" (p. 505). It has been noted earlier that the next generation of teachers should be more racially and ethnically mixed and there are presently numerous policy initiatives to achieve this goal.

A number of researchers (McCarthy & Apple, 1988; Ogbu, 1978) relate that the educational research on minorities requires special attention and different approaches. For example, if one begins to examine educational achievement longitudinally by age, the results will be inevitable, i.e., fewer minorities will have achieved high social and occupational roles. Since some contend (and many operate on the assumption) that individuals secure social and occupational roles due to educational attainment, and that educational attainment is tempered by family backgrounds, individual abilities etc., different approaches to research are in order.

Ogbu (1978) offers that "real motives for minority-group education are not to be discovered in the rhetoric of school people." He contends, "Such motives are better discovered by studying the positions of adult members of the minority group" (p. 25). Although Ogbu's comments relate to grasping formal education and its relationship to minorities, the same thinking can be adopted for probing minority teachers' perceptions on teaching, i.e., ". . . are the motives of formal education [teaching] the same for the minority and the majority groups?" (p. 26).

Additionally, justification for studying on racial/ethnic grounds may also be borrowed from feminist literature. If, as Casey and Apple (1989) contend, studying the profession with a gender-sensitive eye reveals broader and more useful data for restructuring, then the cultural orientation of the profession is an essential factor in the equation.

New reforms that fail to recognize the cultural backgrounds of the teaching force will be as flawed as earlier attempts at school and instructional innovation that omitted gender considerations. If, as Ogbu's (1975) research suggests, members of certain racial/ethnic groups were raised to have distinctly different motives for formal education, then it is only natural to assume that they will teach the basic knowledge of their discipline, within the limits of their organizational and curricular practice, but with a different set of directives for their students on what to do with such knowledge and information.

Menlo, Marich, Evers and Fernandez (1986) note that few recommendations for change in education have been developed directly from first-hand cross-cultural data. Although they reference England, West Germany and the United States, the same accusation can be directed at any one country that represents several or more cultures. Conjecture allows that the failure of many educational programs is a result of the inability or unwillingness of researchers to examine the profession across or through racial/ethnic grounds rather than in separate layers or with special programs to address idiosyncrasies of a particular culture or group.

Although they hold substantial knowledge and insights, minority professionals are seldom involved in developing educational programs that are designed to assist children of their own cultural group. Lisa Delpit (1986) offers one possible reason for so little input from Blacks, Hispanics

11

and other minority groups in reform discussions is that the "language" used is inappropriate and does not recognize the value to be gleaned from minorities in an existing structure. Translation of minorities' "languages" is important since as Jiobu (1988) notes, "The American ethnic scene consists of a potpourri of racial, cultural, religious, and geographic groups and although a given explanation might account for one group, it usually cannot account for very many other groups" (p. 3).

Common Methods of Analysis

One can only speculate that the reason race and ethnicity are left unattended in the literature when issues relative to gender, religion and income are addressed is fear or ignorance—fear of repercussions for tampering with the democratic creed that all people are created equal, or ignorance that even though all people are created equal, goodness can only be found in values and principles emanating from the White, Anglo-Saxon Protestant ethic. Delpit (1988) contributes to this theory when she describes liberal educators' use of the "culture of power" stating ". . . either by virtue of their position, their numbers or their access to that particular code of power of calling upon research to validate one's position, the White educators had the authority to establish what was to be considered 'truth' regardless of the opinions of the people of color . . ." (p. 284).

There are merits in breaking this pattern and teachers have a major role to play. Grant and Sleeter (1988) cite school staff as the primary malefaction in the low academic achievement (in a longitudinal study) of 24 junior high school students from various racial/ethnic backgrounds. "The school could also have taught more explicitly about race, class and gender. What the school did was to treat all students as much alike as possible, while teaching a watered-down version of traditional White, male-dominated curriculum" (p. 38).

Students are much better off when family, community and especially teachers are versed in and share knowledge of racism, sexism and the socioeconomic culture. Just as Grant and Sleeter contend that students, particularly lower-class and/or minority students, would be inclined to challenge the low academic expectations of the school if staff had shared such knowledge, Comer (1989) also calls for greater involvement of teachers. "Preservice programs—in and outside the discipline of education—should provide all students with an understanding of how structural forces, policies, and practices impact communities, groups and families, and child development" (p. 360).

Educating practitioners to transmit such knowledge is not an easy task. To a certain extent, multicultural research on teaching and teacher education tends to rely on real and perceived observations of minority

12

groups in the classroom. However these observations are typically reported in a comparative mode, i.e., how does the minority student's action or performance differ from the majority student's? Possibly a better, more promising approach would be to examine the minority student's behavior and performance in and of itself, probing deeper into that student's inherent background and culture.

This approach also requires that researchers examine educational issues from a community perspective as well as from within the school. Eisenhart (1989), when explaining the concept of "cultural patterns" in multicultural education, argues that patterns learned at home and in the community are viewed as sometimes congruent and sometimes conflicting with the cultural patterns expected and promoted at school. This is an inevitable occurrence since minority groups' cultures are not those upon which the education community bases any knowledge, skills or pedagogy. Resolution is further complicated when minority groups differ with each other in many of the same ways that they differ with the majority population. For instance, there is rare recognition of how different customs and languages are between Indochinese immigrants and Chinese Americans, between members of the Cherokee and Sioux communities or between Black Americans and Haitian immigrants—groups which are often more diverse with each other than they are with the majority culture and language.

Researchers have used a number of different approaches in distinguishing racial/ethnic minorities, all of which appear to borrow in various degrees from economics, political science, sociology and anthropology. One consistent and fairly logical approach is to relate or assign these groups to categories which, on a very basic level, describe how and why they have come to this particular nation, and to what extent they have or have not assimilated into the social, economic and, key to this discussion, educational structures.

According to Jiobu (1988), assimilation can have two major impacts on the societal structure. In one, the majority group is not required to adjust or necessarily recognize the value of the minority group(s); the ethnic group loses its distinction and becomes like the majority. In the second scenario, the majority and minority groups blend together in a melting pot, each loses its distinction and a unique product results. He contends that "... these concepts have their origin partially in scientific theory, partially in utopian wish, and partially in political ideology" (p. 6).

It should be noted, that while some authors question the desirability of assimilation, many (Jiobu, 1988; Ogbu, 1987; Parsons, 1965) conclude that assimilation by certain racial/ethnic groups is nearly impossible given the current social and economic order. Since the primary purpose of this discussion is to examine closely the various types of individuals who comprise the teaching profession, then assimilation, or the extent to which minority teachers become invisible within the profession, will be a minor issue. After all, "cultures differ both in the criteria prescribed for actual performance of specific roles and in the prescribed methods by which individuals come to occupy such roles" (Ogbu, 1978, p. 17). In addition, "An individual's occupation, even one which is traditionally associated with a particular ethnic group [such as Blacks in teaching], tells us little about a person's assimilation (Jiobu, 1988, p. 10).

Just as there are a number of differences between and among racial and ethnic groups in the nation, there are some common indictments, especially from the majority population, shared by these groups. The notion of "genetic deficit," now politely termed as "cultural deficit," is something that has and continues to plague all groups at certain periods in their settlement and assimilation in the nation (Erickson, 1987). As DeLoria (1978) points out, the "cultural deficit" theory enabled frustrated educators to put the blame for school failure outside the school and onto the socioeconomic and political problems of the community. But this is like a vicious circle since as Erickson (1987) makes clear, all aspects are intertwined and inseparable.

In general education, racial and ethnic groups also share a discriminatory approach to their educational needs. Any program or curriculum that is designed to suit particular needs and/or comfort levels, e.g., bilingual education, is considered remedial or less valuable than that which is suited to the majority population. This attitude is perpetuated by teachers who have been trained by the majority culture. Most often these teachers understand and acknowledge no other "right" approach than their own. Given the persistent national concern for a competitive edge in the world economy, for social order and the demographic realities of this country, it is naive to perceive a quality education for any child that is developed by a parochial educational system and delivered by a homogeneous teaching force.

The current mode of inquiry that attempts to identify effective teachers uses the traditional minority model as a gauge. It is tricky. For instance, it is very difficult to discern whether an individual who has been identified as a master teacher and who happens to be a member of a minority group has been so designated because he or she emulates the majority disposition and approach in a significant way or because he or she brings unique contributions from a particular racial/ethnic culture. Thus conditions, experiences and resulting attitudes and approaches of Black, Hispanic, Asian and Native American teachers are of primary concern in this discussion. A greater understanding of these factors may lead to identifying inherent or transferable knowledge and skills that are most effective with students of diverse populations.

The time is appropriate for studying by race/ethnicity for no other reason than to move forward. Such studying need not be judgmental, but

14

certainly it can be descriptive, avoiding the pitfalls delineated by Feiman-Nemser and Floden (1986) earlier. Society is changing and as Bell (1976) notes, "[the] political conditioning of the direction of our work may simply be a rational way of adjusting it to the needs felt in the society in which we live and work" (p. 4).

III

The Teaching Population: Present and Future

G iven the current level of attention and energy devoted to school reform and improvement, a quality education for all children is a reasonable expectation for the coming years. In order to accomplish this goal the content and format of knowledge taught must be culturally responsive, and the teacher will be primarily responsible for its delivery. Who are the individuals who will be presented with this challenge? For the most part they are well-educated White women, dedicated to the profession but unfamiliar with the ethos of the major racial/ethnic cultures of this society. If all teachers will be required to educate effectively all children, then it seems only just to include in the ranks of the profession educators of color who are most familiar with and skilled in the mission. A more culturally diverse teaching force will require significant adjustments to the educational attainment patterns of Black, Hispanic, Asian and Native American youth, as well as a new and more attractive profile of the profession.

The Current Teaching Force

According to Gerald, Horn, Snyder and Sonnenberg (1989), approximately 2.3 million teachers were employed in public elementary and secondary schools in fall 1988 and the demand is expected to rise to 2.5 million by fall 1993. Approximately 10 percent of today's teaching force is Black, Hispanic, Asian or American Indian. However, increases in the number of minority school-aged children dwarf their presence.

The teaching profession has been dominated by females of all racial/ethnic groups for well over a century. White males' greatest representation in the profession was in 1879 when they constituted 42.8 percent of the teaching force (Everden, Gamble & Blue, 1933). Data indicate that males' greatest representation (34.2 percent) within the past 25 years was in 1971, a year that was also the most productive year for education degrees in the century (NEA, 1988; ASCUS, 1988).

17

Differences in teachers' academic preparation are evident in data collected by the National Education Association (NEA) for the report, *Status of the American Public School Teacher* (1988). The data show that in 1961, 14.6 percent of U.S. teachers had less than a bachelor's degree and the highest degree held by 61.9 percent was a bachelor's degree. Twenty-five years later, in 1986 only .3 percent of teachers had less than a bachelor's degree and the majority (50.7 percent) of teachers had a master's degree.

Currently, minority teacher degree attainment appears on par with that of majority teachers. Specifically, a bachelor's degree is the highest degree held by 51.6 percent of minority public school teachers and 48.0 percent of White teachers; 40.6 percent of minority and 46.5 percent of White teachers hold master's degrees. Significantly, 2.3 percent of minority K-12 teachers hold doctorates, while 0.5 percent of Whites have accomplished the same (NEA, 1987). Perhaps this is an indication of minority exclusion from other avenues open to the majority population with higher degrees.

The NEA survey notes a 10-year decrease of teachers under age 30, and an increased percentage of teachers aged 40 to 49 in 1986 (p. 73). Haggstrom et al. (1987) also note the aging teaching force with the proportion of teachers in the 20-24 year old age group dropping from 45.0 percent in 1976-77 to 10.2 percent in 1983-84, and the proportion younger than 35 dropping from 53.2 percent to 37.2 percent.

The graying teaching force is consistent with the national demographic trend toward an older America (see Chapter V); however, it is inconsistent with demographic projections for racial/ethnic minority groups that are expected to increase, through births, well into the next century. Consequently, while fewer minority students are entering teaching careers, the current labor force is aging more rapidly than in the past, depleting the current supply of educators during a period of greatest need.

If, as Rury (1989) notes, age is the most consistent change in the social characteristic of the teacher of the 1980s, then gender may well be the single most important demographic factor influencing the character of the profession. As Lortie (1975) provides, the "ecology of schools" matches the circumstances of women (particularly those married) who teach. In addition, neighborhood schools make it easier for women to economize on travel time and the temporal ecology of schools (five-day weeks, short days, numerous holidays and long summer vacations) provides more time for household duties than available in other occupations. This same schedule, according to Lortie, may be viewed as a subsidy for males in the profession, allowing time for second jobs.

Lortie also suggests that motivation for pursuing teaching is gender related. He notes that the subjective warrant, i.e., what an individual *thinks* is required for success in a given role, comes closer to matching

18

feminine than masculine ideals as defined by our society, and it empha-
sizes qualities that are more widely reinforced for girls than for boys.
According to Hudis (1977), the conflicting priorities of home and work
have a substantial impact on nearly every aspect of women's labor market
behaviors. In a summary of related research, she reports that commit-
ments to a husband and/or children reduces the probability of women
working in any given year; diminishes the extent of their lifetime work
experience; decreases their annual extent of employment, even when they
do choose work; impedes their occupational advancement; and reduces
their earnings (p. 126).

Although both White and minority women have more occupations
open to them today than they did 15 years ago and they participate in the
labor force at a much greater rate, they still maintain primary responsibility for child rearing. There have been many recommendations for restructuring schools, however most refer to internal adjustments in staffing
patterns and roles that will not permeate the basic operational structure
that has typified what the public knows as the school day. Thus, the
general labor requirements that encourage or support female participation
in teaching will likely maintain teaching as a viable career option for
women, in general, in the foreseeable future.

The profession's appeal appears to vary by race and ethnicity, however. Considering that a greater proportion of Black and Hispanic families
are headed by single women, and Black women provide a greater level of
financial support to two-salary households, economic realities dictate that
when minority women enter higher education they are likely to pursue
and subsequently work in professions that will yield greater incomes
than those offered by teaching. In 1987, families with a female head of
household were 13 percent of White families, 23 percent of Hispanic
families and 43 percent of Black families (Bureau of the Census, 1988a).
Further, Black female-headed families are expected to increase by 25
percent by the year 2000. It should be noted that the significant increase
in single-parent families among Blacks is primarily attributed to educated
Black women. High school dropouts accounted for only 6 percent of these
families formed from 1970-1985 while college-educated Black women
comprised 35 percent (Hill, 1989).

Another issue that relates to minority female participation is the
cultural orientation that has been maintained within the present society.
For example, the Hispanic tradition (in reality not unlike those of any
other population group) that dictates the male as provider is evident in
the comparatively low proportion of Hispanic women in the work force.
As Jimenez-Vasquez (1980) provides, women in Hispanic America started
to acquire higher education as preparation to be better housewives and
mothers.

19

It is clear that the nation's school systems continue to employ a significant proportion (24 percent) of all adult females with college degrees and 23 percent of all minorities with college degrees (Darling-Hammond et al., 1987). However, this finding should be viewed within the context of occupational type, especially for Blacks and Hispanics. Participation rates in 1980 for full-time employees in public elementary and secondary schools suggest that Blacks, but particularly Hispanics, were employed in noncertified and noninstructional job classifications. For instance, in 1980, Hispanics were 2.6 percent of all elementary school teachers, 1.7 percent of secondary school teachers, 2 percent of principals and 2.5 percent of central office administrators. At the same time, they comprised 8 percent of schools' unskilled labor, 5.9 percent of service workers and 4.4 percent of clerical/secretarial staff (Orum, 1986).

Prospects for the future teaching force are both encouraging and discouraging. On a positive note, for the 10-year period 1976-86, white-collar, nonclerical occupations increased by slightly more than half and the number of women and minorities in these occupations skyrocketed. Unfortunately, teaching did not benefit from this boom, experiencing a growth rate of only 20 percent of other white-collar, nonclerical occupations (Darling-Hammond et al., 1987). On the other hand, since 1986, teacher education has experienced a boom of its own, with enrollments escalating by as much as 60 percent. If it were not for the notable absence of racial and ethnic diversity (less than 10 percent) a celebration might be in order (Dilworth, 1989; AACTE, 1989b).

The Future Teaching Force

Minority representation in white-collar occupations such as teaching is dependent to a great extent on the participation of these groups in post-secondary education; the high school completion rate for the new work force, 18-24 year olds, is disheartening. In 1985, American Indian youth had the lowest completion rate (60 percent), followed by Hispanics (62 percent), Blacks (75 percent), and Whites (83 percent) (Mingle, 1987). More recent reports for this age group indicate that the completion rate for the 18-24 year-old age cohort has improved more for Blacks than for any other racial/ethnic group and that while Hispanics have made gains, they continue to lag behind both Blacks and Whites (ACE, 1990; Bureau of the Census, 1987, 1988a,c).

Although larger percentages of Blacks and Hispanics are completing high school now than 10 years ago, smaller percentages of these graduates are enrolling in college. Their four-year college completion rates, along with American Indians, are significantly lower than the White population's. Moreover, they are more apt than the majority population to postpone college entrance, attend a two-year college first and attend college part-

20

time. Of particular note is the high proportion of Hispanics (55.3 percent) and American Indians (56.7) who attend two-year institutions (ACE, 1988a; Woods & Williams, 1987). Thus, as Mingle (1987) contends, the success of minorities in gaining access to professional fields hinges upon their ability to gain admission to the upper-division programs of four-year institutions. However, the two-year completion and four-year transfer rates of most students are not high. Citing C. Dennis Carroll's *High School and Beyond* (HS&B) longitudinal data, Mingle reports that only 9 percent of 1980 high school graduates entering community colleges directly after graduation were seniors in college four years later.

There are a number of socioeconomic factors that influence participation and completion of a baccalaureate degree, particularly in what is considered the typical length of time, four to six years. Unfortunately, Blacks', Hispanics' and American Indians' training and experiences generally place them at higher risk of failing to complete this educational cycle. For example, family income, parents' education, type of high school (e.g., public v. private) all contribute to the profile of college students. High school graduates who come from families with incomes of less than $20,000, whose parents have less than a high school diploma and who studied a general curriculum at a public high school are not likely to enter any postsecondary institution (Mingle, 1987, p. 19). That minorities are disproportionately classified in one or more of these groups clearly indicates the gravity of the situation. What once was considered normal in enrollment and completion of higher education is no longer applicable to the majority of the minority population.

Those high school graduates who immediately enter college full-time and continue without "dropping out" or "stopping out" are now considered on the "fast track." Mingle (1987), in his report of Carroll's HS&B analysis, identifies significant differences among fast-track students by race and ethnicity. He reports Asians "overwhelmingly ahead" of other groups in this category with 1 of every 3 students persisting to completion in four years. This is compared to 1 of 5 Whites, 1 of 7 Blacks, 1 of 10 Hispanics and 1 of 12 American Indians reaching that goal. The tendency to take more than four years to complete a four-year baccalaureate program is consistent for teacher education students, who on the average need four and a half years to complete four-year programs (AACTE, 1987b).

Minority student participation in education decreases as students proceed through the pipeline. Postsecondary minority representation is only a fraction of K-12 representation and the proportion of college students pursuing teaching as a career is miniscule. According to one 1987 survey, the average college of education enrolls approximately 400 students. Of this number, only 22 students will be Black, 7 Hispanic, 3 Asian and 2 American Indian/Alaskan Native. Less than 10 percent of

21

prospective teachers are members of any non-European group, while approximately 30 percent of the K-12 population comes from these groups (AACTE, 1988).

The findings of the 1987 "Pipeline" survey are consistent with the racial/ethnic demographic and educational profile of the nation. For instance, the survey found that the western region of the nation enrolls the greatest proportion of minorities in teacher education, which is consistent with the significantly high Hispanic, Asian and Native American populations in California, Hawaii, New Mexico and Oklahoma. It also concludes that historically Black institutions (HBIs) continue to produce Black teachers beyond their expected capacity. Located in the southern region, home of 56 percent of Black Americans, the 113 HBIs matriculate approximately 17 percent of Black students enrolled in postsecondary education. HBI schools of education enroll about 30 percent of Black teacher education students. Tribal colleges that are controlled by American Indian communities also make a significant contribution to the training of teachers. For example, Oglala Lakota College (SD), one of the very few baccalaureate-level institutions of this type, has increased the number of Native American teachers from one to approximately 100 in recent years (Carnegie Foundation for the Advancement of Teaching, 1989).

Researchers have offered a number of reasons for the increasingly low participation of minorities in the teaching profession. Primary malefactions cited include: students' preference to enter into professions with higher salaries and more prestige; increased use of teacher competency examinations that disproportionately affect minorities; lack of sufficient financial aid incentives; and the shrinking pool of minorities enrolled in four-year colleges and universities (Alston, 1988; Dilworth, 1986; Garibaldi, 1987; Smith, 1987). Darling-Hammond et al. (1987) examined career choices of Blacks, Hispanics, Asians and American Indians. They report, as do others (ACE, 1987), that since 1975 women and minorities have increased participation in the fields of business, science and health-related fields at the expense of education and the social sciences.

As Table 1 shows, degrees in education earned by minorities declined precipitously from 1977 to 1985, with the greatest proportionate decrease being for Black graduates (58 percent). Degrees awarded in education also declined for Asians (14 percent) and Native Americans (32 percent) during this seven-year period; the number of degrees increased and subsequently decreased for Hispanics (17 percent).

The inability of the profession to attract and retain a critical mass of newly qualified minority teachers portends difficulties in future decades for all sectors of education. The professoriate in schools, colleges and departments of education is also deplete of minority representation leaving very little optimism for culturally informed training of prospective teachers (AACTE, 1987b; Harvey & Washington, 1989).

22

Table 1. Number and Percent of Bachelor's Degrees Conferred in Education by Race/Ethnicity 1977–1985

	1977		1979		1981		1985		CHANGE
	N	%	N	%	N	%	N	%	%
White, non-Hispanic	125148	87.2	108949	86.6	93724	86.6	77531	88.3	−38.0
Black, non-Hispanic	12992	9.1	11509	9.1	9494	8.8	5456	6.2	−58.0
Hispanic	3050	2.1	3029	2.4	2847	2.6	2533	2.9	−17.0
American Indian/Alaskan Native	707	—	645	—	569	—	483	—	−31.6
Asian/Pacific Islander	894	—	785	—	723	—	770	—	−13.9
Nonresident Alien	741	—	869	—	908	—	1015	1.2	+36.9
TOTALS	143532		125786		108265		87788		−38.8

Source: *The Condition of Education*, Volume 2 Postsecondary Education (1989). Washington: USED/OERI pp. 78–80.

The shortage of minority educators has not gone unnoticed. Recruitment and retention programs have been established in all regions of the country; however, some have met with more successes than others. The effectiveness of these activities is contingent upon a number of factors including genuine concern, commitment of resources and the ability to collaborate with educational and community institutions and agencies that are most knowledgeable and skilled in meeting the needs and desires of the target groups (AACTE, 1989a).

Finally, those involved in recruitment efforts must recognize that the profession reflects more disincentives for people of color than for others. Testing requirements for entry, exit and certification far exceed those of other bachelor-level fields and minorities understand that these examinations typically present a greater challenge to them. Although teacher salaries have improved over the years (AFT, 1989) there is a general perception of a low cost-benefit ratio for the field. Since Blacks and other minorities attend college with greater loan burdens than others (Kirshner & Thrift, 1987; ACE, 1990) and minority women carry greater responsibility for household income than their majority peers, the decision to enter teaching is often a sacrifice. The educational community has not offered individuals of color compelling reasons to join its ranks. The often cited reward of being a "positive role model" is inadequate for most. It suggests that external physical appearance is more valued than internal knowledge. If Black, Hispanic, Asian and Native Americans have reasonable assurance that they will be trained, employed and compensated well, consulted with and promoted for their unique contributions, the field will certainly be more attractive.

IV

Motivation, Rewards and Incentives

There are basic and widely accepted notions about what motivates an individual to enter the teaching profession and about the rewards and incentives one gleans from participating in it. Certain of these factors appear to be standard to teachers of all backgrounds, while others suggest differentiating appeal across racial/ethnic groups. A cross-cultural understanding of motivation can do much to enhance recruitment efforts while rewards and incentives provide a good point of reference for retention strategies.

Motivation

The literature on motivation as it relates to teaching is extremely consistent regardless of nationality, socioeconomic background, gender or point in time. It is a foregone conclusion that prospective and practicing teachers enter the profession with the altruistic motive of helping youth and society. An example of this thinking is found in the results of surveys conducted in 1961 and 1985 of teacher education students at Northern Illinois University (Joseph & Green, 1986); of teachers responding to Lortie's (1975) "Five Towns" survey in the early 1970s; of Singapore student teachers in 1965, 1981 and 1988 (Soh Kay Cheng, 1989); and of Black, Hispanic and Asian American teacher education students from all regions and socioeconomic backgrounds in 1988 (AACTE, 1990). In all instances, the decision to enter teaching is primarily prompted by the noble gesture of service, rather than by material gain.

Joseph and Green (1986) attempt to put the question of motivation in perspective when they state: "Suspicions about self-reported motives expressed by researchers and educators suggest that the literature on teacher motivations should not be accepted at face value" (p. 31). The authors found reasonable evidence that motivation in teaching may be a learned response which masks deep neurotic impulses or provides a mechanism for saving face. For example, those who pursue teaching may well have an underlying desire for superiority or perceive an occupation working with children more comfortable (especially to women) or less threatening than working with adults.

One motive often cited is that teaching provides an opportunity for individuals from blue-collar backgrounds to move to white-collar jobs. While some researchers (Sedlak & Schlossman, 1987; Sykes, 1983; Dworkin, 1980) provide convincing evidence that the desire to teach is conditioned more by the heretofore limited access to other occupations than by aspirations to become part of another class, it can be argued that teaching was the only available vehicle for women and minorities to an upper class. The motive of class mobility appears to be subject to socioeconomic conditions more so than others and as a result has greater implication for minority participation than do others.

Dworkin (1980) offers an interesting perspective of the class mobility of teachers by race/ethnicity. In a study of urban Black, White and Chicano teachers in the Southwest from 1930-1970, he found that younger (under 35) Black and White teachers are more often from families where the head of household is in a high-status occupation than are older teachers (36 and above). On the other hand, young Chicano teachers are more inclined to come from blue-collar and lower occupational origins than their more senior counterparts. He notes that this exception is likely as Chicanos, more recently than Blacks, have been able to utilize education as a vehicle for upward mobility.

Dworkin suggests that since the 1930s teaching has been frequented by the children of individuals in high occupational strata and that children of blue-collar parentage participate at a greater rate during times of teacher shortages. He argues against the generally accepted notion that the "class structure had become more permeable, enabling individuals from working-class and farm backgrounds to enter public school teaching" (p. 71). It should be noted that those individuals who were "young" during Dworkin's 1970 study, are now part of the emerging older cohort and the premise that young White and Black teachers come from professionally classed families and Chicanos from blue-collar may no longer be credible.

More recent data (NEA, 1987) suggest that there has been a significant increase in the percentage of teachers whose fathers are professionals or semiprofessional, from 14.5 percent in 1961 to 21.9 percent in 1986. However, 22.5 percent of minorities, compared to 7.2 percent of Whites, report fathers who are unskilled laborers. Similarly, while 22.2 percent of White teachers report manager or self-employed fathers, only 15.5 percent of minorities report the same. In addition, minority teachers are more inclined to have parents completing less than both an elementary and a high school education.

Indeed, there have been some changes in the character of teaching, and of individuals pursuing teaching, in the past decade; generally, new

26

teachers are older, spend more time preparing to teach and can expect to earn more money initially than their predecessors. Although women continue to dominate the profession, education is no longer the field of first choice for minorities or for the general undergraduate population (ACE, 1987).

A 1988 survey of teacher education students (AACTE, 1990) indicates that significant proportions of new Black, Hispanic and Asian American teachers likely come from lower-income families. Specifically, the survey reveals that approximately 31 percent of Asian, 20 percent of Black and 14 percent of Hispanic teacher education students come from families with an estimated income of less than $15,000. Approximately 12 percent of White students report parental incomes at this level. Teacher education students coming from families with an estimated parental income of $15,000-$30,000 are also generally perceived as low-income. Approximately 51 percent of Hispanic, 36 percent of Black, 27 percent of White and 13 percent of Asian teacher education students fall in this category. The proportion of education students coming from families of middle- and upper-income brackets ($30,000 or more) shows White students coming from markedly better financial circumstances (60 percent) than Blacks (45 percent), Asians (56 percent) and Hispanics (35 percent).

It is interesting to compare the economic background of those pursuing teaching with those entering a more prestigious occupation such as medicine. An Association of American Medical Colleges study (1989) of students accepted in medical school in fall 1988 provides some measure for comparison. There appear to be considerable differences in the economic backgrounds of teacher education and medical students by race/ethnicity. For instance, 31 percent of Asian American teacher education students report low family incomes of less than $15,000 but only 7 percent of Asian American medical students indicate the same. Approximately 4 percent of White medical students' family economic backgrounds fall in the low-income category, while 12 percent of teacher education students do. Black (15 percent) and Hispanic (ranging from 11 percent to 25 percent, by group) new medical students cite higher rates of poverty than do teacher education students. (See Table 2.)

Parental educational attainment also contributes to the demographic profile of new teachers. For the most part, the parental educational backgrounds of teacher education students' mirror those of the nation as a whole. Specifically, approximately 56 percent of Hispanic students report mothers with less than a high school education compared to 39 percent of Asians, 24 percent of Blacks and 14 percent of Whites. Similarly, approximately 47 percent of Hispanic education students report fathers with less than a high school diploma compared to 26 percent of Blacks, 24 percent of Asians and 17 percent of Whites (AACTE, 1990).

Table 2. Percent of Teacher Education and Medical Students from Low-, Moderate-, and Upper-Income Families, by Race/Ethnicity

Income Less Than $15K	% Teacher Education Students	% Medical Students
White	12	4
Black	20	15
Hispanic	14	—
Mexican	—	16
Puerto Rican (Mainland)	—	22
Puerto Rican (Commonwealth)	—	25
Other Hispanic	—	11
Asian	31	7
Native American	—	19

Income—$15K–$30K	% Teacher Education Students	% Medical Students
White	27	9
Black	36	17
Hispanic	51	—
Mexican	—	22
Puerto Rican (Mainland)	—	13
Puerto Rican (Commonwealth)	—	21
Other Hispanic	—	13
Asian	13	10
Native American	—	19

Income Greater Than $30K	% Teacher Education Students	% Medical Students
White	60	50
Black	45	34
Hispanic	35	—
Mexican	—	36
Puerto Rican (Mainland)	—	36
Puerto Rican (Commonwealth)	—	32
Other Hispanic	—	42
Asian	56	43
Native American	—	36
Source:	(AACTE, 1990)	(AAMC, 1989)

NOTE: These data represent two distinctly separate surveys, designs and analyses. Teacher education data reflect responses of students *enrolled* in 1988–89 academic year. Medical student data reflect percent of *applicants* for 1988. Totals may not equal 100% because of rounding and exclusion of *Nonresponse* category. A (−) in table indicates data unavailable.

Understanding that most white-collar jobs require at least a high school diploma, and that most also pay salaries above $15,000, it is safe to assume that a significant proportion of Black, Hispanic and Asian teacher education students come from blue-collar and/or low-income families. This cursory review is insufficient to conclude that teaching is

28

currently considered a vehicle to permeate a particular socioeconomic class by any group. However, it does suggest that the poor of all groups continue to have reasonable access to the teaching profession, more so than to professions such as medicine. In addition, those of middle- and upper-class backgrounds continue to pursue careers in teaching.

Access to higher education clearly tempers the number and type of individuals entering teaching. As noted earlier, minorities' low participation rates in four-year institutions limit access to a number of occupations, including teaching. On the other hand, Lortie (1975) suggests that such inequities work to the advantage of the teaching profession. He states:

> Few occupations are in as good a position to take advantage of socioeconomic constraints which limit access to college education. The system of inexpensive and accessible colleges for teacher training turns out to be more than an institution of socialization—it also recruits. One finds a kind of 'entrapment' as such colleges draw in students of limited opportunity whose initial interest in teaching is low (p. 48).

Nevertheless, he concedes, and the research literature suggests, if limited opportunity tempers initial interest it operates in a gentle and benign way.

Changes in higher and teacher education within the past decade also counter the easy access notion. The requirements to enter and exit teacher education institutions have increased substantially. What were once four-year programs now generally require an additional semester's work; five-year programs to allow for additional field and induction experiences are becoming more common; and nearly every state requires a certification examination for beginning teachers (AACTE, 1987a,b).

Rewards and Incentives

The motivation to enter teaching is somewhat useless without something to sustain it. For the teaching profession these sustaining components are termed "rewards and incentives" and they play a key role in the level of satisfaction that teachers derive from their work. "Rewards" and "incentives" are typically used interchangeably in the literature. Although they are closely related they can be differentiated in that "incentives are rewards that are anticipated on the condition that their potential recipients take particular action" (Kottkamp, Cohn, Provenzo, & McCloskey, 1987, p. 22). Rewards are commonly categorized as extrinsic, ancillary and intrinsic. While extrinsic rewards, such as salaries, are objective and are received in detachment from the process of work itself, intrinsic rewards are subjective and are received wholly while engaged in the work itself. Ancillary rewards such as income security draw on objective characteristics of the work, but may also be subjectively valued more by some than by others (Kottkamp et al., 1987, p. 19).

As the previous discussion on motivation suggests, teachers universally garner more gratification from intrinsic rewards such as the fulfillment of having successfully contributed to the development of a child, than from extrinsic rewards such as compensation and position. Yet, in their study of Black, Cuban and White teachers, Kottkamp et al. found differences among groups in general satisfaction; receipt of various types of rewards; orientations toward colleagues and individuals in authority positions; and desire to teach certain types of children. The authors found that Black and Cuban teachers, more than others, gain primary satisfaction through intrinsic rewards, especially when they have the opportunity to study, plan, master classroom management, "reach" students and associate with colleagues and children. The authors also noted that approximately one-quarter of White respondents choose ancillary rewards at a rate 10 percent greater than Cuban teachers and three times that of Black teachers.

Kottkamp et al. (1987) approached this particular study with two questions: whether the receipt of rewards and incentives takes a similar or different pattern across ethnic groups; and whether interactions between the teacher and his/her principal or students enhance the understanding of receipts beyond the knowledge of ethnic identity of the teacher alone. Since their study, "Teacher Ethnicity: Relationships with Teaching Rewards and Incentives," is unique in its analysis on a racial/ethnic dimension, it will be used to frame the remainder of the discussion.

A simple, yet deceiving indicator of satisfaction with the rewards of teaching is length of service. Since adults with appropriate training are free to move in this society from one occupational situation to another, the presumption is that those who remain in teaching obtain adequate benefits from it. In addition, individuals who do leave teaching, likely do so perceiving less risk of difficult re-entry than those in other occupations.

The sheer number of schools in this country gives qualified teachers the impression that they will be able to return to teaching, if they need to, at almost any time and in almost any place in the country. However, the research of Wise, Darling-Hammond and Berry (1987) suggests that there is increasing diversity in the recruitment, selection and hiring practices of school districts throughout the nation that impedes an easy entry, exit and re-entry process for teachers. This finding is somewhat substantiated in NEA (1987) survey data that indicate fewer teachers are being hired than in previous decades and higher percentages of teachers are remaining in their current systems (p. 21).

NEA (1987) found that 4.6 percent of all teachers report two years or less of teaching experience; 44.8 percent had from 3 to 14 years of full-time teaching experience; and fully half of all teachers (50.8 percent) had 15 or more years. The mean number of years of full-time teaching experience in 1986 was 15 years (p. 20). While approximately 50 percent of teacher education students indicate that they intend to pursue teaching for 10 or more years (AACTE, 1990), research data (Metropolitan Life, 1988) also suggest that the majority (55 percent) of new and less experienced minority teachers are more likely to say that they will probably leave the profession within the next 5 years (p. 21).

Although Kottkamp et al. (1987) did not use years of service in the general satisfaction equation, the demographic profile of their respondent group provides some insights and reflects Dworkin's teaching population profile of the 1970s. Specifically, Kottkamp et al. reported that Blacks and Whites have comparable proportions of experience, most ranging from 6 to 20 years and that Cubans in teaching, generally reflective of the Hispanic population, tend to have a range of fewer and greater years of experience when compared to the others. NEA (1987) data also show that Black and other minority teachers are less likely to have breaks in service for any reason than their majority counterparts (p. 22).

A more direct and thus reliable gauge of teacher satisfaction is practitioners' responses to the following general questions: How satisfied do you feel about your particular job/career? (Kottkamp et al., 1987 and Metropolitan Life, 1988) School? (Kottkamp et al., 1987) How willing would you be to teach again? Metropolitan Life has surveyed teachers on satisfaction since 1984 and reports in 1988 that 50 percent of teachers are "very satisfied" with their job, which is a substantial increase for the period. However, the NEA (1987), surveying educators since 1961, reports a significant decrease in teachers that "certainly" or "probably" would teach again and an increase in the percentage of teachers who would not.

Both national surveys, the NEA and Metropolitan Life, found that minorities and/or younger teachers are more inclined to be dissatisfied with the profession than older, more experienced professionals. The NEA study notes, however, that in 1981 and in 1986, younger teachers (under 30) were reporting their certainty of becoming teachers again in roughly the same proportion as their over-age-50 cohorts (p. 59).

On the other hand, Kottkamp et al. (1987) in their survey of Dade County, Florida, teachers found that Whites on the whole were less satisfied with their jobs and schools than Blacks and Cubans. Specifically, they report "a tendency for Anglo teachers to be the least satisfied with their jobs and schools and the most likely to send their own children to a private rather than public school if given the option" (p. 14). It is interesting to note however that Dworkin (1980), in his study of teachers in a southwestern urban district, found no significant differences in the desire to quit teaching among urban Black, White and Chicano educators of the same occupational origins in the 1970s (p. 72).

As would be expected, neither salary (Kottkamp et al., 1987) nor job security (NEA, 1987) has been identified as having a great influence on a teacher's decision to remain in the profession. Only 16 percent of Whites,

31

11 percent of Blacks and 12 percent of Cubans stated that their salary provided the most satisfaction for them. On the other hand, Cubans (40 percent) were more likely than Whites (21 percent) and Blacks (31 percent) to consider "respect from others" a reward of teaching (p. 16).

Regardless of its perceived limited influence, satisfaction typically is tied to working conditions and compensation. According to the NEA, since 1981, teachers working in small school districts seem more satisfied with their careers than those in large- and medium-sized districts (p. 59). This suggests rewards beyond compensation in that teachers in urban and suburban school districts have higher mean salaries than those in smaller systems (Metropolitan Life, 1988, p. 12; NEA, 1987, pp. 66-67).

Kottkamp et al. (1987) provide a category of analysis termed "negative rewards," i.e., detractors from positive intrinsic and extrinsic rewards. They report that low salaries, discipline problems and, to a lesser extent, burnout are the most frequently cited deterrents or negative rewards for all racial/ethnic groups. Among teachers of different backgrounds, the authors found Black teachers perceived more problems with discipline, Cubans were frustrated when unable to achieve their own ideals and Whites were burned out more than others. (See Table 3.)

It is interesting to note that in a different survey (AACTE, 1990), when prospective teachers were asked why more minorities are not entering the profession, responses were similar across groups. As Table 4 shows, minority students, and Black students in particular, find low

Table 3. Teachers' Top-Ranked Reasons Why Teachers Are Leaving the Classroom, by Race/Ethnicity

| | (In Percent) | | |
	White	Black	Cuban
Low Salaries	73	75	68
Discipline Problems	62	75	60
Burnout/Exhaustion	44	26	34
Frustration	25	17	28

Source: Kottkamp et al. 1987

NOTE: Kottkamp et al. asked practicing teachers to *rank* among 10 items reasons why teachers are leaving the profession.

Table 4. Prospective Teachers' Reasons Why Minorities Are Not Entering Teaching, by Race/Ethnicity

| | (In Percent) | | | |
	White	Black	Hispanic	Asian
Low Salaries	44	74	62	53
Discipline Problems	23	53	43	41
Burnout/Exhaustion	12	29	30	41
Frustration	27	42	32	47

Source: AACTE, 1990.

NOTE: AACTE's Metropolitan Life survey asked teacher education students to *select* among 8 items reasons why minority students are not entering the profession.

32

salaries and discipline in the schools to be detractors more so than do Whites. On the other hand, White students do not cite burnout/frustration at as high a rate as their professional cohorts. Frustration in being unable to achieve one's ideals is perceived to be a deterrent to professional entry by Black and Asian students more so than by Whites and Hispanics.

These differences in perceptions may be attributed to a number of factors related to actual experience in teaching, teaching environment and/or socioeconomic background. Certainly, each group best represents the views of its peers. Consequently, it may be safe to infer that higher teacher salaries will help retain practicing teachers of any group and will specifically help recruit minorities.

Discipline problems in the schools are clearly a reality that many prospective White teachers do not seem to anticipate or comprehend. Since the majority of White teacher education students come from predominantly White rural and suburban schools and neighborhoods, and wish to return to these situations, this lack of comprehension is conceivable. Conversely, minority students who frequently attend urban and low-income schools, often associated with disciplinary problems, may view the teaching experience in a different light (AACTE, 1990).

Since, as discussed earlier, Black and Hispanic women make greater contributions to total family income than do White women, the need to work may be so compelling that burnout and frustration are not feasible or likely reasons for quitting a job. In a study of Black and White women's commitment to work and wages, Hudis (1977) finds that Black women place a primary emphasis on maximizing income. White women may make job decisions that reduce the importance of maximizing income and emphasize instead ancillary rewards such as desirable working hours, commuting distance or other job characteristics that may conflict with higher wages (p. 141).

Minority teachers are more inclined to see the societal benefit of teaching, in their initial decision to teach and in their present purpose (NEA, 1987). Additionally, according to Kottkamp et al. (1987), 24 percent of majority teachers find "the economic security, time, freedom from competition and appropriateness for persons like me" more important than do Cuban teachers (15 percent) and Black teachers (9 percent) (p. 19).

One very interesting difference among teachers is their perceptions of peers and colleagues. According to Kottkamp et al. (1987), Anglo teachers are oriented more toward collegial or peer relationships than are Black teachers. Conversely, Black teachers have more favorable views of principals and are more disposed towards individuals in formal authority positions than are their majority peers (p. 28). This attitude may be partially explained when considering the Metropolitan Life finding that minorities are more critical of their colleagues than others. The study

33

reports that they feel their peers have "minimal expectations for teaching and learning"; "show little expertise and personal knowledge in lecture material"; and "go through the motions of presenting information" (p. 27).

In addition, minority groups' experiences in this country have forced them to rely upon authority and bureaucracy when serious conflict arises. It is consistent therefore for Blacks, Hispanics, Asians and American Indians to appeal to school or building authority, i.e., the principal, than to their majority peers who are not required by law or inference to be fair and equitable.

Finally, in their examination of incentives, Kottkamp et al. (1987) devised a congruency quotient that approximated one-third of teachers actually teaching the kinds of students they prefer. Students, the authors state, are "powerful agents" for the distribution of incentives and disincentives. Students have a wide range of latitude in deciding to work with, fight against or ignore the teacher's efforts to reach and teach them. The authors' calculations suggest that Black teachers, as a group, would probably be able to derive the highest amount of incentive value from the student populations that they currently teach, while White teachers, as a group, likely would derive the lowest incentive value. Since "incentives are rewards anticipated on the condition that their potential recipients take particular actions" (p. 22), and intrinsic rewards, such as student achievement, are vital to satisfaction for teachers of all groups, this finding is particularly important.

The previous discussion suggests that teachers of all backgrounds share a common desire to help children grow and develop. However, the decision to pursue this desire occupationally—initially and over time—is often more costly for people of color. As the role of the teacher is redefined in school restructuring efforts, it will be useful to gauge the extent to which changes complement a multiethnic teaching force.

V

Racial/Ethnic Cultures

The following discussion does not provide a complete description of the non-European racial/ethnic groups present in this country but does offer a cursory review of the demographic and educational experiences of those groups that will most likely be evident for the balance of this century. This short journey attempts to provide a sense of the rich, cultural texture of this society, and of the nation's schools.

There is a growing recognition among informed educators that groups typically termed "minority" actually represent the majority in a significant number of localities. Although certain states and regions of the nation have not experienced drastic changes in the composition of their populations, the fact remains that the complexion of the United States is changing. At present, approximately 14 percent of all adults and 20 percent of all children are members of minority groups, and within the next two decades one-third of all school-aged children will fall into this category. In addition, "minority workers will make up one-third of the net additions to the U.S. labor force. By the turn of the century, 21.8 million of the 140.4 million people in the labor force will be non-White" (ACE, 1988b).

For these very basic reasons, the educational needs of the racial/ethnic groups of this and coming decades are significantly different than those of previous years. In this increasingly technological era, it is essential that education be truly functional for these groups rather than a ceremonial testament to social justice and equal educational opportunity. Part of the solution, if indeed not all, lies in a true or greater understanding of the ethos of the major racial/ethnic groups in this country, an identification of effective teaching methods and formats, and a determination of the processes whereby this information can be translated to all teachers.

Minority Groups

The experiences of minority groups in this country vary by country of origin, language, primary settlement areas and purpose for being in those areas. The majority of the U.S. population arrived as European immigrants. Other groups were already settled (Native Americans) or were absorbed as part of territorial acquisition (Pacific Islanders). The Black population arrived in servitude. The resultant educational inequities have been well documented in the literature. As the largest and most visible non-European ethnic group in this country, most of the efforts to improve, enhance or equalize educational opportunities in the nation have been designed for and directed to Black Americans. Asian Americans, specifically Chinese and Japanese, follow the latter group in arrival and, at the beginning of this century, in number. Their experiences have been tempered (more so than for Blacks) by world economy, but they do share discriminatory experiences based upon visible differences in appearance.

Hispanics, in the numbers they represent today, are the most "recent group" and share the language barriers of Asians. Hispanics are the youngest and fastest growing minority in the nation. Between 1980 and 1987, the Hispanic population increased by 30 percent compared to 6 percent for non-Hispanic groups. Individuals of Mexican origin (11.8 million) are by far the largest Hispanic group in the country followed by Puerto Ricans, Cubans, Central and South Americans.

The following provides a profile based on census projections of the U.S. population in the coming decade:

- The Hispanic, Black and Asian population under age 18 will increase from 21 percent to 34 percent (Schwartz & Exter, 1989).
- The number of Americans aged 25 to 34 will fall 15 percent. The proportion of Whites in this age group will drop from 74 percent to 68 percent; Blacks will increase from 13 to 14 percent; Hispanics from 10 to 14 percent and Asians from 3 to 5 percent.
- The number of Americans aged 35 to 44 will increase by 18 percent. The proportion of Whites in this age group will drop from 78 to 73 percent; Blacks will increase from 11 to 13 percent; Hispanics from 8 to 10 percent and Asians from 3 to 4 percent.
- The number of 45 to 54 year olds will increase by approximately 50 percent. The proportion of Whites in this age group will decrease from 80 to 77 percent; Blacks will increase from 10 to 11 percent; Hispanics from 7 to 8 percent and Asians from 3 to 4 percent (Staff, 1989).

Race/Ethnicity and Assimilation

According to Jiobu (1988), ethnicity can be real and ephemeral, insignificant and important. He describes "symbolic ethnicity" wherein there is recognition of one's heritage and culture, e.g., St. Patrick's Day, yet the group is so well assimilated into the society that on March 17 "...it is said, that there are only two kinds of people, the Irish and those who want to be" (p. 11-12). Allen and Turner (1988a) note, "For Whites born in the United States an ethnic identity is usually less important than it was a half century ago, but much of its current meaning may be subtle and personal rather than readily visible to strangers" (p. ix). There is, according to Gans (cited in Jiobu, 1988), "nostalgic allegiance" to the culture of the immigration generation, or that of the old country.*

Social and economic realities of this country dictate a different disposition towards ethnicity for non-European groups. Discrimination against minorities in housing, employment and educational opportunities is easier to accomplish since the targets have clearly visible physical, and to a lessor extent, language distinctions. Non-European residents cannot voluntarily dismiss their ethnicity as easily as many European groups (Jiobu, 1988). Albeit, recognizing that many individuals from these groups would likely decline the opportunity, such a dismissal would probably escalate the cultural synthesis of the educational enterprise.

Jiobu (1988), in his examination of California's Asian, Mexican and Black Americans' assimilations, offers five areas of commonality in their U.S. experiences:

1. the size of a minority group has little to do with the intensity and scope of the majority reaction;
2. the specific ethnicity or race of a group has little to do with the intensity and scope of the majority reaction;
3. antiminority forces subordinated all groups through the establishment of a legal infrastructure which at times also rendered economic restrictions;
4. violence accompanied the building of the infrastructure; and
5. pejorative stereotypes developed (p. 56).

Jiobu also probes and analyzes the demographic factors of sex, age and fertility to establish a "demographic potential" quotient. He defines demographic potential as "certain features of a group's demography that predispose the group toward socioeconomic achievement" (p. 77). Although the concept of a racial/ethnic group's advancement being premised on such ordinary factors is narrow, Jiobu offers some basic facts that, on their face, have particular relevance to the education of minorities in general, and to occupational choice (teaching) in particular. While the author's conclusions are based upon 1980 census data for eight California

*NOTE: The broad anatomical categories of race: Caucasoid, Mongoloid and Negroid are more convenient than they are accurate. The majority of individuals, particularly in this nation, can not legitimately be assigned to one single category without a significant application of exceptions. "There are Whites who are darker than some Negroes; dark hair and eyes are common among all races..." (Benedict in Marden & Meyer, 1968). Consequently, discussion that focuses on ethnicity or ancestry will yield more useful descriptions. It should be noted, however, that certain minority groups "see their position in society as qualitatively different from that of White ethnic groups. They prefer to describe the primary dimension of society in terms of race rather than ethnicity" (Allen & Turner, 1988a, p. ix).

groups (Black, Chinese, Filipino, Japanese, Korean, Mexican, Vietnamese and White), one may be reasonably confident that the trends are consistent with the general U.S. population.

Much of the recent attention to minorities and their education has been prompted by the visible evidence of many Black, Hispanic and Asian youngsters in the classroom and by the statistical projections, conservative or otherwise, that promise an even greater presence. Demographers, of necessity, approach populations in a pedantic way and utilize graphic pyramids to illustrate different factors in the population. Generally, an "expansive" pyramid indicates a population with many young people (a broad base) and systematically tapers to a point (few older persons). In a "stationary" pyramid, the middle portion is narrower than the base or top indicating a zero or slow growth population; and the "constrictive" pyramid depicts few youngsters (narrow base), a bulging mid-portion, and moderately tapering top (p. 63).

Jiobu suggests that a constrictive classification can be advantageous to the group's economic progress. He finds that Black, Chinese, Japanese and White Americans are constrictive. Filipino, Korean and Vietnamese Americans are somewhat stationary and Mexican Americans expansive. Although populations with few youths at their base cannot maintain the same size over time, fewer children free resources from child rearing to direct consumption and economic endeavors. Jiobu further offers that women in constrictive populations may be more able to pursue work outside of the home given a relatively small cohort of children (p. 67).

In regard to gender, Jiobu finds Chinese Americans with the most balanced population, 99 males per 100 females; followed by Filipinos (97:100), Whites (97:100) and Blacks (96:100); Vietnamese (108:100) and Mexican American males (105:100) outnumber females. A number of socioeconomic factors seem to contribute to these imbalances in the U.S. population. Aside from natural biological occurrences (a longer expected life span for women in the Western society), high infant mortality rates for groups such as Blacks, selective migration as in the case of Mexican Americans and the Vietnamese, and restrictive immigration laws that earlier had an impact on Chinese and Filipino entrance, have influenced the representation of men and women from racial/ethnic groups (pp. 68-69).

A group's growth is also greatly influenced by the fertility of its female population. As has been reported by Hodgkinson (1986) and others, the non-White population of the nation is growing at a greater rate than is the majority population. Jiobu (1987) offers child-women ratios (number of children four years or younger per 100 women aged 15 to 44 years) for California population groups, which are consistent with these reports. While he finds Japanese (17:100) and Korean (24:100) American rates lower than those of Whites (25:100), the larger ethnic populations, i.e.,

Mexican (53:100), Vietnamese (37:100), Black (34:100), Filipino (31:100) and Chinese (27:100), show high fertility (pp.73-75). Fertility is influenced by a number of factors that reflect a group's culture: religious doctrine that prohibits birth control; familial upbringing that discourages young women from pursuing higher education or work outside the home.

Although educational attainment and geographic residence and mobility significantly influence the type of work individuals pursue, population growth, sex composition and age constructs significantly impact rate of participation. Theoretically, population groups with constrictive pyramid structures should have a critical mass of mature, established, "active" members that can potentially maintain or improve that group's socioeconomic status. At the same time, this creates a "job squeeze" for the young as they compete for a limited number of similar jobs or attempt new markets (Jiobu, 1988). Of course for U.S. racial and ethnic minorities, the status quo is wholly unacceptable. For groups such as Blacks, the critical mass of mature members are losing ground rather than improving their socioeconomic status. Moreover, their youths are not pursuing jobs traditionally supported by members of their own population, such as teaching. It should be noted, however, that Blacks' participation in the profession was initially approved and supported as a means to maintain segregated schools. Although de facto segregation prevails at present, the necessity of maintaining a critical mass of Black teachers no longer seems as crucial to the majority as well as to the Black population as it once was.

Expansive or growing populations, such as Hispanic Americans, entering the teaching profession would not create a "job squeeze" for their older cohort but could create one for their White cohorts. Neither Hispanics nor Asians have a long-standing tradition in the teaching profession. Consequently, in acknowledging ample numbers of potentially "active" Hispanic youth, less than full participation in teaching, now and in the future, can only be attributed to discrimination in educational opportunities and recruitment or failure to permeate the profession's infrastructure.

Since the primary purpose of this presentation is to become more familiar with the current experiences of individuals of various groups, the following discussion does not attend to issues relative to racism per se, but rather to basic demographic information regarding general perceptions of these groups. Data are provided for the four major racial/ethnic groups: Black, Hispanic, Asian/Pacific Islander and American Indians/Alaskan Native.

Black Americans

Black Americans, approximately 27 million, comprise the largest racial/ethnic minority group in the country. Black Americans carry the distinction of being the only minority group counted separately in census data as far back as 1820. It is the only group that came to America en masse involuntarily—and enslaved. While common knowledge holds that Black people in the U.S. share a similar heritage through Africa and in bonding fostered by enslavement, this is not altogether accurate. Indeed, while the majority, 90 percent, of individuals identifying themselves as African Americans are descendents of involuntary immigrants, a significant proportion of Black Americans today are voluntary immigrants. Between 1983 and 1986, over 20,000 individuals migrated from Jamaica to join close to one-quarter million individuals with Jamaican ancestry already living in the United States. Haitian immigration has been twice as high as it was in the 1970s and Black individuals from the Dominican Republic, East and West Africa, Guyana, Trinadad-Tobago, the British West Indies and a host of Central and South American countries continue to settle in this country, work and send their children to public schools (Allen & Turner, 1988b).

As of 1988, the majority, approximately 56 percent, of the Black population live in the southern region of the country; however, the balance of U.S.-born Blacks, and the majority of Black immigrants (57 percent) reside, for the most part, in the major metropolitan areas of the nation. Blacks constitute 28 percent of the total population of the South, 10 percent in the Northeast, 9 percent in the Midwest, and 5 percent in the West. "Blacks in 1980 comprised about 24 percent of the population in central cities, up from only 12 percent in 1950 and 20.6 percent in 1970" (p. 149). On the other hand, Black presence increased in the suburbs between 1970 and 1980 at a rate almost three times that of Whites (Allen & Turner, 1988a; Bureau of the Census, 1989).

Although the majority of U.S.-born Blacks share a common heritage in African, and subsequently in the nation's southern tradition, those raised in northern, western and central regions likely have adopted unique approaches to life and living that reflect the experiences of their ancestors as well as their own. Understanding that subtle and sometimes blatant forms of discrimination persist throughout the nation, it is a fair assumption that most Black people in America have shared the experience of isolation and discontent that is characteristic to that condition.

Similarly, Black people in all regions share the historical and continuing handicap of being a disproportionately low-income group. Approximately 33 percent of the U.S. Black population was below the poverty level in 1987. The poverty rate for Black families is more than three times that of White families (8 percent); and about 46 percent of Black children under the age of 18 in families, compared with 15 percent of White children, are poor. Unemployment in the Black population 16 years old and over, is twice that of the White population (Bureau of the Census, 1988a, 1989).

40

Between 1978 and 1982, the income for Black people declined in all regions of the country. The drop was so drastic in the Midwest that it replaced the South as the region where Black incomes were lowest and racial inequality was highest. Since that time, the income of U.S. Blacks has improved in all regions of the nation. However, there has been no progress in attaining family income parity and "significant erosion" has occurred in all regions other than the South, and especially in the Midwest (Swinton, 1989).

The displacement of Black Americans and other non-European minorities that positions them at the bottom rung of the economic ladder has implications in a number of vital areas that are not always fully acknowledged by educators. For instance, Achtenberg and Marcuse as cited in Calmore (1989) point out, "Housing, after all is much more than shelter: it provides social status, access to jobs, education, and other services, a framework for the conduct of household work, and a way of structuring economic, social, and political relationships" (p. 79).

Although data show a significant number of businesses owned by Blacks, Hispanics and Asians, such enterprises are disproportionately concentrated in industries with limited growth potential, e.g., beauty/barber shops, food and apparel stores and gas stations. They are also typically located in the central cities. While such businesses provide services and jobs, 60 percent of Black employers report that their work force is 75 percent to 100 percent minority. These institutions have made a significant impact on the education of Blacks. Without their contribution, Blacks' educational attainment would probably not be what it is today.

As they have in the past, Black churches maintain colleges and universities, as well as day care and other support services, that allow educational growth for children and their families. The Black Church may be defined as "the historic Black communions or denominations which are independent of White control, and which maintain their own structures of governance, finance, ritual, worship, and outreach" (Lincoln, 1989, p. 137). Approximately, 84 percent of Black Christians in the United States are affiliated with or were raised in the Methodist, Baptist or Pentacostal faith. In addition, there is a growing presence of Blacks in the Muslim faith. The Black Church is a very significant component of the Black cultural experience and any future research in attitudes and perceptions should probe for its influence.

Hispanic Americans

Hispanic Americans share the distinction of being both the oldest and newest immigrants to the United States. Mexican Americans were the first "immigrants" to this country in the sixteenth century and also repre-

41

sent the largest group of post-1970 settlers in the country (Allen & Turner, 1988a).

The term *Hispanic American* is even more generic in its description of individuals than is *Black American*. The term describes persons of Mexican, Puerto Rican, Cuban, Central and South American, and Spanish descent. There are 19.4 million Hispanic Americans and the population has grown approximately 34 percent between the 1980 census and 1988 (Bureau of the Census, 1989).

Individuals of Hispanic ancestry reside in all regions of the nation and are concentrated by subgroups. For instance, in 1980, 75 percent of Mexican Americans lived in California or Texas, approximately 50 percent of mainland Puerto Ricans were in New York and 60 percent of Cuban Americans lived in Florida. In 1988, 63 percent of Hispanics lived in Arizona, California, Colorado, New Mexico and Texas, with 55 percent of all Hispanics living in California or Texas. New York (11 percent), Florida (8 percent), Illinois (4 percent) and New Jersey (3 percent) also have significant numbers of Hispanic Americans. Approximately 90 percent of U.S. Hispanics resided in nine states and are more urbanized (87 percent) than any other group (Orum, 1986; Bureau of the Census, 1989).

Orum (1986) indicates that the apparent large growth of Hispanics, particularly in the 1980 census, is due to several factors: undercounting by up to 40 percent in the 1970 census, a comparatively lower median age and higher proportion of women of child-bearing age and the slower decline in birthrates than the White and Black populations. Because of their large and growing immigrant presence, as well as language differences, Hispanic Americans experience discrimination that thrives on issues other than physical appearance. In certain areas, there is a presumption on the part of others that a Hispanic individual is "an illegal" until or unless he or she proves otherwise. In truth, as the "youngest" population group in the nation, three-fourths of Hispanic Americans are native-born. In addition, significant numbers are naturalized citizens or legal immigrants with resident alien status or legal refugees (Orum, 1986, p. 11). The U.S. Bureau of the Census and others provide allowance for undocumented immigration of Hispanics; however, there is a general consensus that these individuals are undercounted more often than any other U.S. population group.

Most Hispanics speak both English and Spanish, although past isolation of this group allows for a greater rate of native language retention (Orum, 1986, p. 12). Because there is a critical mass of Hispanics in the K-12 population requiring bilingual instruction and services, the general population tends to ignore the English proficiency of Hispanic Americans.

As with other non-European minorities, Hispanic families earn substantially less than White families, and the gap is not narrowing. The incidence of poverty among Hispanic children in 1984 was above that for

42

all U.S. children. Of the 1.1 million Hispanic families that were living below the poverty level in 1986, 49 percent were maintained by a woman with no husband present. In a trend typical to all other population groups, families with heads of households who had completed less than four years of high school constituted 62 percent of the Hispanic families below the poverty level in 1986 (Orum, 1986; Bureau of the Census, 1987).

Hispanic employment patterns are different from those exhibited by Whites and Black Americans, and are significantly different by subgroup population. Labor force participation rates for Hispanic men are higher than those for other groups of men. Over 80 percent of Hispanic men 16 years and older were either working or seeking work in 1985, as compared to 77 percent of White men and 71 percent of Black men. Hispanic women, however, report the lowest employment-population ratios of all groups. The Hispanic unemployment rate is typically 60 percent above the White rate in both good and bad economic times, but is about one-third below the Black rate. Puerto Rican Americans generally have the lowest labor force participation and Mexican Americans the highest (Orum, 1986).

It appears that much of the difference among Hispanic groups may be attributed to the regional allegiance of certain groups. For instance, Mexican Americans who are densely populated in the Southwest have a significant number of nonskilled labor positions available to them. Puerto Rican Americans, on the other hand, who were initially lured to the Northeast by industry have since been displaced through economic depression, plant and factory closings (Allen & Turner, 1988a).

Hispanic entrepreneurs tend to fair better than their Black and Asian peers. For instance in 1982, Hispanic-owned firms generated $15 billion in receipts versus $12.4 billion for Black businesses and $14.5 billion for Asian-owned firms (Allen, 1989). According to the 1980 census, Hispanic Americans were at least as segregated from Whites in housing as Asian Americans but not as isolated as Blacks (Jaynes & Williams, 1989).

Asian Americans/Pacific Islanders

People of Asian and Pacific Island ancestry may be the most heterogeneous of the major racial/ethnic groups in the United States. Those identified as Asian Americans come from or are descendents from Asia, Europe and other parts of the world. As of 1980, there were approximately 800,000 Chinese; 710,000 Japanese; 775,000 Filipino; 355,000 Korean; 262,000 Vietnamese and 362,000 Asian Indian Americans. Individuals from Cambodia, Laos, Thailand, Pakistan, Samoa and Guam are also included in statistics on Asian Americans.

According to Allen and Turner (1988b), immigration from Asia (which includes the Middle East and Pacific Islands) has risen so dramatically that the Census Bureau's estimates of the number of U.S. residents of a

43

race other than Black or White increased 45 percent between 1980 and 1986. Immigrants from the largest Asian countries first arrived in either California (San Francisco was the primary reception area) or Hawaii in the nineteenth century, mostly to work as miners, general laborers or agricultural workers. Asians provided a cheap labor force, particularly in California, well into the twentieth century (Allen & Turner, 1988a). Generally speaking, Asians remain concentrated in the western Pacific corridor, New York City and Hawaii. They are slightly less urbanized and segregated in housing than are Black and Hispanic Americans.

As with other immigrant populations, the experiences of those arriving in the United States during the first half of this century were different from the experiences of those arriving within the last two decades. The differences derive to a greater or lesser extent from the political and economic conditions of the times. Voluntary immigrant groups, and to a certain extent, nonvoluntary groups, are or have been subject to periods of conscious inclusion efforts, primarily to meet labor imperatives. Subsequently, they have been excluded when there is no longer a need, or when the group threatens to accumulate more power or wealth than the dominant group.

This inclusion/exclusion paradigm is apparent in the experiences of many Asian as well as Hispanic groups. For instance, Chinese Americans were initially welcomed in the mid-nineteenth century to build the nation's railroad and to assist California gold miners with their domestic needs. As these immigrants appeared able to compete in mining with the majority, as the Japanese eventually did in agriculture, they were barred through legislation from becoming naturalized citizens and thus barred from land ownership, voting, military service and other rights and privileges (Joibu, 1988).

Asians were essentially excluded from immigration to this country by a series of laws which were not amended until 1965. Until then quota systems were in effect that strongly favored immigrants from northern and western Europe. Since 1965, the immigration of people from Asia has increased dramatically with particularly large flows of Chinese, Filipinos, Koreans and Asian Indians (Joibu, 1988; Allen & Turner, 1988a). Data indicate that these new immigrants are better educated and established than those arriving earlier in the century. This is likely the result of the new laws that allotted additional spaces for people in certain occupations.

For political reasons, the Vietnamese in America have had a markedly different reception than have other Asian immigrant groups. After the fall of Saigon in 1975, the federal government actively supported Vietnamese immigration, established support mechanisms and purposely promoted their settlement in various parts of the country rather than in one region. Vietnamese immigrants arriving since 1975 are also atypical of earlier

44

Asian immigrants in their socioeconomic background with an estimated 68 percent holding white-collar jobs prior to their migration.

Asian Americans own 21 percent of minority-owned businesses, generating approximately $14.5 billion in receipts in 1982. Their average sales and receipts exceed Black-owned businesses; however, those of certain subgroups, i.e., Vietnamese, Filipinos and Hawaiians, have average receipts that approximate those of Black Americans (Allen, 1989).

American Indians/Alaskan Natives

Possibly because of their relatively small representation, less than 1 percent of the U.S. population, American Indians/Alaskan Natives are commonly perceived as a vanishing group. On the contrary, 1980 census data indicate a 72 percent increase although several methodological and economical factors likely contributed to this phenomenal growth (Allen & Turner, 1988b; Bureau of the Census, 1988c). This group's population pyramid is more expansive in appearance than constrictive or stationary and the group is growing at twice the rate of the nation as a whole.

The approximately 1.4 million American Indians identify closely with tribes and bands. Only two tribes, Cherokee (16 percent) and Navajo (11 percent), have more than 150,000 members. The Sioux, Chippewa and Choctaw claim more than 50,000 persons each, and the Pueblo, Iroquois Confederacy, Apache, Lumbee and Creek reported at least 25,000 persons per group. According to the 1980 census, six tribes have a population ranging from 10,000 to 25,000 persons and 90 percent of approximately 500 tribes and bands have populations of less than 10,000 (Bureau of the Census, 1988c).

The Alaskan Native population is comprised of three groups: Eskimos (53 percent), American Indians (34 percent) and Aleuts (13 percent), totaling approximately 64,000 persons. This group's population growth is similar to that of the larger American Indian community in that almost half of its members are under 20 years old. The Alaskan Native population is currently identified by legally established "regional corporations," i.e., geographically bound corporate boundaries organized to conduct business for profit (Bureau of the Census, 1988c).

The majority of American Indians live in states west of the Mississippi River (California, Oklahoma, Arizona, New Mexico) and in North Carolina. Other states with populations of 38,000 or more are Washington, South Dakota, Michigan, Texas and New York. Federal relocation and migration assistance programs, instituted during the 1950s, encouraged significant numbers of American Indians to move from their typically rural reservations to urban centers, e.g., Los Angeles, San Jose, Denver, Salt Lake City, Dallas, Chicago, Minneapolis and Cleveland. Although two-thirds of U.S. states have reservations, approximately 50 percent of American Indians live in urban areas and one-third live on reservations (Bureau of the Census, 1988c; Allen & Turner, 1988a).

While this group can legitimately be referred to as "first Americans," they are, on all terms, considered a racial/ethnic minority and suffer from similar segregation in education, employment and housing. McDonald (1989) reports that Indian poverty and unemployment rates are among the highest in the nation with median family income nearly 50 percent less than that of the national norm and a reservation poverty rate of nearly 50 percent (p. 2).

VI

Conclusions

The nation's demographic imperative suggests that the prevailing perceptions of teachers' backgrounds, attitudes and motivations be re-examined. Black, Hispanic, Asian and Native American teachers are similar in many ways to their majority peers, but are advantaged in their ability to know and communicate in more than one culture. It is this ability that shows much promise for devising educational methods and curricula that can make a difference in the academic achievement of the nation's increasingly diverse student population. Unfortunately, the typical profile of the nation's teaching force does not adequately couple socioeconomic factors such as race and ethnicity with an individual's decision to enter and remain in the profession or with that individual's approach to educational practice.

There are several possible reasons for this. First, the literature suggests that there is much more to be learned about the practice of teaching than there is of its practitioners. The questions, What needs to be taught? and How should it be taught? take precedence over the equally important question, Who will complete the task? Second, teaching is a necessary service occupation, dominated by females, and controlled by and large by the public sector. As a consequence, it does not garner the same level of interest and support as do male-dominated, professionally controlled occupational fields. Third, in this democratic society, there is a reluctance to probe for differences between and among various racial/ethnic backgrounds, as such probing counters the "melting pot" theory.

Educational research that includes race and ethnicity as a variable is typically comparative in nature. These studies often do not go far enough in helping educators understand or identify the best means and methods to educate individuals from various groups. The same restriction exists in studies of teachers. For instance, it is difficult to discern what skills, knowledge and ability minority teachers may bring to the classroom that accentuate learning for students of their own group. Consequently, it is virtually impossible to incorporate these factors into teacher training for the benefit of all teachers.

Although there are efforts to increase the number of minority teachers in the work force, the data indicate a less than 10 percent minority

47

representation in the field for the next decade. While this is not dramatically different from the composition of the teaching force throughout this century, it has major implications when coupled with simultaneous and rapid minority K-12 population growth.

The next generation of teachers appears to have the same altruistic notions about the profession as their predecessors. However, it will be particularly difficult to sustain the interest and motivation of new minority teachers over long periods of time. Data indicate that these teachers state intentions to leave sooner than others, tend to come from poorer backgrounds and carry a greater level of family income responsibility than their majority counterparts. In essence, new minority teachers will not remain in the profession long enough to help build a solid pool of experienced educators. Clearly, today's Black, Hispanic, Asian and Native American teacher education students have made a conscious choice to join the profession, overlooking competing and more prestigious career options. However, improved working conditions and compensation will be essential in the maintenance of a multicultural teaching force.

The responsibility for establishing a culturally mixed and culturally informed teaching population weighs heavily on those with the authority to direct recruitment policies and programs and the ability to research, design and implement programs and curricula. This does not exonerate practicing professionals in the classroom and the academy from expanding their views on cultural diversity with the assistance of parents and the community. To shape an educational experience that reflects the best of this society will not be an easy task. Nonetheless, it is a necessary one and it is possible.

References

Acker, S. (1989). Rethinking teachers' careers. In S. Acker (Ed.), *Teachers, gender and careers* (pp. 7-20). London: Falmer Press.

Allen, J. (1989). Minority business performance: A comparison among ethnic groups. *Focus, 17*(5).

Allen, J. P. & Turner, E. J. (1988a). *We the people: An atlas of America's ethnic diversity.* New York: MacMillan.

————. (1988b). Immigrants. *American Demographics, 10,* 23-27.

Alston, D. A. (1988). *Recruiting minority teachers: A national challenge.* Washington, D.C.: National Governors' Association.

American Association of Colleges for Teacher Education. (1987a). *Minority teacher recruitment and retention: A public policy issue.* Washington, D.C.: AACTE. ED 298123

————. (1987b). *Teaching teachers: Facts and figures, 1987.* Washington, D.C.: AACTE. ED 292774

————. (1988). *Teacher education pipeline: SCDE enrollments by race and ethnicity.* Washington, D.C.: AACTE. ED 305346

————. (1989a). *Recruiting minority teachers: A practical guide.* Washington, D.C.: AACTE.

————. (1989b). *Teaching teachers: Facts and figures, 1988.* Washington, D.C.: AACTE.

————. (1990). *AACTE/Metropolitan Life survey of teacher education students.* Washington, D.C.: AACTE.

American Association of Medical Colleges. (1989). *Minority students in medical education.* Washington, D.C.: AAMC.

American Council on Education. (1987). *Minorities in higher education 6th annual status report.* Washington, D.C.: ACE. ED 299844

————. (1988a). *Minorities in higher education 7th annual status report.* Washington, D.C.: ACE.

————. (1988b). *One-third of a nation.* Washington, D.C.: ACE. ED 297057

_____. (1990). *Minorities in higher education 8th annual status report.* Washington, D.C.: ACE.

American Federation of Teachers. (1989). *Survey and analysis of salary trends: 1989.* Washington, D.C.: AFT.

Anderson-Levitt, U. M. (1987). National culture and teaching culture. *Anthropology and Education Quarterly, 18,* 33-37. EJ 351817

Association for School, Colleges and University Staffing. (1988). Teacher supply and demand in the United States a look ahead. *ASCUS Research Report.*

Bell, D. (1976). *The cultural contradictions of capitalism.* New York: Basic Books.

Berliner, D. C. (1986). In pursuit of the expert pedagoge. *Educational Researcher. 15,* 5-13.

Bureau of the Census. (1987). *The Hispanic population in the United States: March 1986 and 1987 (advanced report).* (Series P-20, No. 416). Washington, D.C.: U.S. Department of Commerce. ED 286696

_____. (1988a). *Money income and poverty status in the United States: 1987 (advanced data).* (Series P-60, No. 161). Washington, D.C.: U.S. Department of Commerce. ED 298241

_____. (1988b). *United States population estimates by age, sex, and race: 1980 to 1987.* (Current Population Reports, Series P-25, No. 1022). Washington, D.C.: U.S. Government Printing Office.

_____. (1988c). *We, the first Americans.* Washington, D.C.: U.S. Department of Commerce. ED 304392

_____. (1989). *Population profile of the United States.* (Special Studies Series P-23, No. 159). Washington, D.C.: U.S. Department of Commerce.

Calmore, J. O. (1989). To make wrong right: The necessary and proper aspirations of fair housing. In J. Dewert (Ed.), *The state of Black America* (pp. 77-109). New York: National Urban League.

Carnegie Foundation for the Advancement of Teaching. (1989). *Tribal colleges: Shaping the future of native America.* Lawrenceville: Princeton University Press.

Casey, K. & Apple, M. W. (1989). Gender and the conditions of teachers' work: The development of understanding in America. In S. Acker (Ed.), *Teachers, gender and careers* (pp. 171-186). London: Falmer Press.

Charters, W. W. (1963). The social background of teaching. In N. L. Gage (Ed.), *Handbook of research on teaching* (pp. 715-783). Chicago: Rand McNally.

Chipman, S. F. & Thomas, V. G. (1987). The participation of women and minorities in mathematical, scientific, and technical fields. In E. Z. Rothkopf (Ed.), *Review of research in education* (pp. 387-430). Washington, D.C.: AERA.

Clifford, G. J. (1989). Man/woman/teacher: Gender, family, and career in American educational history. In D. Warren (Ed.), *American teachers: Histories of a profession at work* (pp. 293-343). Washington, D.C.: AERA.

Cochron-Smith, M. & Larkin, J. M. (1987). Anthropology and education: What's the "and" mean? *Anthropology and Education Quarterly, 18,* 38-42. EJ 351818

Comer, J. P. (1989). Racism and the education of young children. *Teachers College Record, 90,* 352-361. EJ 395975

Cunnison, S. (1989). Gender joking in the staffroom. In S. Acker (Ed.), *Teachers, gender and careers* (pp. 151-167). London: Falmer Press.

Darling-Hammond, L. & Green, J. (1988). Teacher quality and educational equality. *College Board Review, 148,* 16-23.

Darling-Hammond, L., Johnson Pittman, K., & Ottinger, C. (1987). *Career choices for minorities: Who will teach?* Unpublished manuscript. National Education Association and Council of Chief State School Officers, Washington, D.C.

DeLoria, V. (1978). The Indian student amid American inconsistencies. In T. Thompson (Ed.), *The schooling of native America.* Washington, D.C.: AACTE.

Delpit, L. D. (1986). Skills and other dilemmas of a progressive Black educator. *Harvard Educational Review, 36,* 379-85.

_____. (1988). The silenced dialogue: Power and pedagogy in educating other people's children. *Harvard Educational Review, 58,* 280-298. EJ 378426

Dilworth, M. E. (1984). *Teachers' totter: A report on teacher certification issues.* Washington, D.C.: Howard University/ISEP. ED 266086

_____. (1986). Teacher testing: Adjustments for schools, colleges, and departments of education. *Journal of Negro Education, 55*(3). EJ 343282

_____. (1989). Recruitment: The good news and the bad news on the teaching profession. In A. M. Garibaldi (Ed.), *Teacher recruitment and retention* (pp. 8-10). Washington, D.C.: NEA.

Dreeben, R. (1970). *The nature of teaching: School and the work of teachers.* Glenview, IL: Scott Foresman & Company.

Dworkin, A. G. (1980). The changing demography of teachers: Some implications for faculty turnover in urban areas. *Sociology of Education, 53,* 65-73. EJ 222558

Eisenhart, M. (1989). Cultural difference and American schools: Rethinking the approach. *Teaching, 1,* 5-15.

Erickson, F. (1987). Transformation and school success: The politics and culture of educational achievement. *Anthropology and Education Quarterly, 18,* 335-356. EJ 365549

Everden, E. S., Gamble, G. C. & Blue, H. G. (1933). *National survey of the education of teachers: Teacher personnel in the United States, Volume II.* Washington, D.C.: U.S. Government Printing Office.

Feiman-Nemser, S. & Floden, R. E. (1986). The cultures of teaching. In M. C. Wittrock (Ed.), *Handbook of research on teaching* (3rd ed). New York: Macmillan Publishing Company.

Fox, R. B. (1961). Factors influencing the career choice of prospective teachers. *Journal of Teacher Education, 12,* 427-432. EJ 040380

Freidus, H. (1989). Gender and the choice of teaching as a second career. Paper presented at the annual meeting of the American Educational Research Association, San Francisco, CA. ED 314360

51

Garibaldi, A. M. (1986). *The decline of teacher production in Louisiana (1976-1983) and attitudes towards the profession.* Atlanta: Southern Education Foundation. ED 268108

_____. (1987). *Quality and diversity in schools: The case for an expanded pool of minority teachers.* Paper presented at the American Association of Colleges for Teacher Education Wingspread Conference on Minority Teacher Recruitment: A Public Policy Issue, Racine, WI. ED 295931

_____. (Ed.). (1989). *Teacher recruitment and retention.* Washington, D.C.: NEA.

Gerald, D. E., Horn, P. J., Snyder, T. D., & Sonnenberg, W. C. (1989). *State projections to 1993 for public elementary and secondary enrollment, graduates and teachers.* Washington, D.C.: NCES.

Gottlieb, D. (1964). Teaching and students: The views of Negro and White teachers. *Sociology of Education, 37,* 345-353.

Gramb, J. D. (1949). Teachers as a minority group. *Journal of Educational Sociology, 22,* 400-405.

Grant, C. A. & Sleeter, C. E. (1988). Race, class and gender and abandoned dreams. *Teachers College Record, 90,* 19-40. EJ 391440

Groff, P. J. (1961a). Personality self images of student teachers. *Journal of Teacher Education, 12,* 433-436.

_____. (1961b). School desegregation and the education of Negro teachers in the south. *Journal of Teacher Education, 12,* 8-12.

Haggstrom, G. W., Grissmer, D. T., & Darling-Hammond, L. (1988). *Assessing teacher supply and demand.* Santa Monica: Rand Corporation. ED 299224

Harvey, W., & Washington, V. (1989). *Affirmative rhetoric, negative action: African-American and Hispanic faculty at predominantly White institutions.* Washington, D.C.: ASHE-ERIC.

Haubrich, V. F. (1960). The motives of prospective teachers. *Journal of Teacher Education, 11,* 381-386.

Hill, R. B. (1989). Critical issues for Black families by the year 2000. In J. Dewart (Ed.), *The state of Black America, 1989* (pp. 41-61). New York: National Urban League.

Hodgkinson, H. L. (1986, May 14). Here they come, ready or not. *Education Week,* pp. 13-37.

Holliday, B. G. (1985). Differential effects of children's self perceptions and teachers' perceptions on Black children's academic achievement. *Journal of Negro Education, 54*(1). EJ 313145

Holmes Group. (1986). *Tomorrow's teachers: A report of the Holmes group.* East Lansing: The Holmes Group.

Hudis, P. M. (1977). Commitment to work and wages: Earnings differences of Black and White women. *Sociology of Work and Occupation, 4,* 123-145.

Jaynes, G. D. & Williams, R. M. (Eds.). (1989). *A common destiny: Blacks and American society.* Washington, D.C.: National Academy Press.

Jimenez-Vasquez, R. (1980). *Social issues confronting Hispanic-American women.* Paper presented at the National Institute of Education Conference on the Educational and Occupational Needs of Hispanic Women, Washington, D.C. ED 194252

Jiobu, R. M. (1988). *Ethnicity and assimilation.* Albany: SUNY Press.

Jordan Irvine, J. (1990). *Black students and school failure: Policies, practices, and prescriptions.* Westport, CT: Greenwood Press.

Joseph, P. B. & Green, N. (1986). Perspectives on reasons for becoming teachers. *Journal of Teacher Education, 37,* 28-33. EJ 350073

Kane, P. R. (1989). *Attraction to teaching: A study of graduating seniors at Columbia College and Barnard College.* Paper presented at the annual meeting of the American Educational Research Association, San Francisco, CA. ED 308140

Kellar, B. (1989). Only the fittest will survive: Black women and education. In S. Acker (Ed.), *Teachers, gender and careers.* London: Falmer Press.

Kennedy, M. (1987). Inexact sciences: Professional education and the development of expertise. In E. Z. Rothkopf (Ed.), *Review of research in education* (pp. 133-167). Washington, D.C.: AERA. ED 285840

Kidwell, C. S. (1988). *American Indians in graduate education.* Unpublished manuscript. Conference on Graduate Education, American Council on Education and Brookings Institution, Washington, D.C.

Kirshner, A. H. & Thrift, J. S. (1987). *Access to college: The impact of federal financial aid policies at private historically Black colleges.* New York: United Negro College Fund/National Institute of Independent Colleges and Universities.

Kottkamp, R. B., Cohn, M. H., McCloskey, G. N., & Provenzo, E. F. (1987). *Teacher ethnicity: Relationships with teaching rewards and incentives.* Unpublished report. U.S. Department of Education, Office of Educational Research and Improvement, Washington, D.C. ED 298078

Lightfoot, S. L. (1987). On excellence and goodness. *Harvard Educational Review, 57,* 202-205.

Lincoln, C. E. (1989). Knowing the Black church: What it is and why. In J. Dewart (Ed.), *The state of Black America* (pp. 137-149). New York: National Urban League.

Lortie, D. C. (1975). *Schoolteacher: A sociological study.* Chicago: University of Chicago Press.

Lubeck, S. (1988). Nested contexts. In L. Weis (Ed.), *Class, race, and gender in American education* (pp. 43-62). New York: SUNY Press.

Maeroff, G. I. (1988). *The empowerment of teachers: Overcoming the crisis of confidence.* New York: Teachers College Press.

Marden, C. F. & Meyer, G. (1968). *Minorities in American society* (3rd ed.). New York: Van Norstrand Reinhold.

McCarthy, C. & Apple, M. W. (1988). Race, class and gender in American educational research: Toward a nonsynchronous parallelist position. In L. Weis

(Ed.), *Class, race, and gender in American education* (pp. 9-39). New York: SUNY Press.

McDonald, D. (1989, August 2). Stuck in the horizon: A special report on the education of Native Americans. *Education Week*, pp. 1-16.

McWilliams, C. (1964). *Brothers under the skin.* Boston: Little, Brown and Company.

Menlo, A., Marich, M., Evers, T. & Fernandez, R. (1986). *A cross cultural comparison of the sources of professional enthusiasm and discouragement in teaching in England, West Germany, and the United States.* Paper presented at the American Educational Research Association Meeting, 1986. ED 266099

Metropolitan Life Foundation. (1988). *The American teacher: 1988.* New York: Louis Harris and Associates.

Mills, J. R. & Buckley, C. W. (1989). *Restructuring predominantly Black schools, colleges and departments of education to accommodate the non- traditional minority teacher candidate.* Manuscript submitted for publication.

Mingle, J. R. (1987). *Focus on minorities: Trends in higher education.* Denver: Education Commission of the States and State Higher Education Executive Officers.

Mitchell, D. E., Ortiz, F. I., & Mitchell, T. K. (1987). *Work orientation and job performance: The cultural basis of teaching rewards and incentives.* Albany: SUNY Press. ED 237488

Nakanishi, O. T. & Hirans-Nakanishi, M. (1983). *The education of Asian and Pacific Americans: Historical perspectives and prescriptions for the future.* Phoenix: Oryx Press.

National Education Association. (1987). *Status of the American public school teacher.* Washington, D.C.: NEA.

Nigris, E. (1988). Stereotypical images of schooling: Teacher socialization and teacher education. *Teacher Education Quarterly, 15,* 4-19. EJ 379398

O'Brien (1984). The commatization of women: Patriarchal fetishism in the sociology of education. *Interchange, 15,* 43-60. EJ 302043

Ogbu, J. U. (1978). *Minority education and CASTE.* New York: Academic Press.

_____. (1987). Variability in minority school performance. A problem in search of an explanation. *Anthropology and Education Quarterly, 18,* 312-334. EJ 365548

Orum, Lori S. (1986). *The education of Hispanics: Status and implication.* Washington, D.C.: National Council of La Raza. ED 274753

Pang, V. O. (1988). Ethnic prejudice: Still alive and hurtful. *Harvard Educational Review, 58,* 375-379.

Parsons, T. (1965). Full citizenship for the Negro American? A sociological problem. In T. Parson & K. Clark (Eds.), *The Negro American* (pp. 709-754). Boston: Beacon Press.

Perkins, L. M. (1989). The history of Blacks in teaching: Growth and decline within the profession. In D. Warren (Ed.), *American teachers: Histories of a profession at work* (pp. 344-369). New York: MacMillan.

54

Pratt, R. (1973). *The public school movement: A critical study.* New York: David McKay Co.

Rury, J. L. (1989). Who became teachers? The social characteristics of teachers in American history. In D. Warren (Ed.), *American teachers: Histories of a profession at work* (pp. 9-51). New York: MacMillan.

Schwartz, J. & Exter, T. (1989). All our children. *American Demographics. 11*, 34-37.

Sedlak, M. & Schlossman, S. (1987). Who will teach? Historical perspectives on the changing appeal of teaching as a profession. In E. Z. Rothkopf (Ed.), *Review of Research in Education* (pp. 93-131). Washington, D.C.: AERA.

Shulman, L. S. (1987). Knowledge and teaching: Foundations of the new reform. *Harvard Educational Review, 57,* 1-22. EJ 351846

Smith, G. P. (1987). *The effects of competency testing on the supply of minority teachers.* Unpublished manuscript. National Education Association and the Council of Chief State School Officers, Washington, D.C.

Soh, Kay-cheng. (1989). *Motives for teaching of female certificate in education students.* Singapore: Institute of Education. ED 310070.

Staff. (1989). Sex, race and ethnicity. *American Demographics, 11,* (Supplement), 3-13.

Swinton, D. (1989). The economic status of Black Americans. In J. Dewart (Ed.), *The state of Black America* (pp. 9-39). New York: National Urban League.

Sykes, G. (1983). Public policy and the problem of teacher quality: The need for screens and magnets. In L. S. Shulman & G. Sykes (Eds.), *Handbook of teaching and policy* (pp. 192-213). New York: Longman.

Thompson, T. (Ed.). (1978). *The schooling of native America.* Washington, D.C.: AACTE.

Tyack, D. B. (1967). *Turning points in American educational history.* Waltham, MA: Blaisdell Publishing.

Warren, D. (Ed.). (1989). *American teachers: Histories of a profession at work.* New York: MacMillan.

Willcox, I. & Beiget, H. (1953). Motivations in the choice of teaching. *Journal of Teacher Education, 4,* 106-107.

Wise, A. E., Darling-Hammond, L., & Berry, B. (1987). *Effective teacher selection: From recruitment to retention.* Santa Monica, CA: Rand Corporation.

Woods, J. E. & Williams, R. A. (1987). *Articulating with two year colleges to create a multiethnic teaching force.* Paper presented at the American Association of Colleges for Teacher Education Wingspread Conference on Minority Teacher Recruitment: A Public Policy Issue, Racine, WI.

About the Author

Mary E. Dilworth is senior director for research at the American Association of Colleges for Teacher Education (AACTE), a national, voluntary organization of colleges and universities that prepare the nation's teachers and other educational personnel. In this position, she is responsible for developing the research agenda of the Association and she directs the activities of the ERIC Clearinghouse on Teacher Education.

She has consulted with many national organizations and educational institutions on issues of equity, particularly in regard to teaching and teacher education. She is the author of numerous articles, reports, and the book *Teachers' Totter: A Report on Teacher Certification Issues.* She is currently editor for an upcoming AACTE publication on restructuring schools of education for diversity.

Index

Academic achievement, xi, xii, 12
Academic expectations, 12
African American, xiv
American Association of Colleges for
Teacher Education
—research data, 31
—surveys, 6, 25, 27
American Indians/Alaskan Natives,
45–46
—census data, 45
—federal relocation, 45
—geographic residence, 22, 45
—income level, 46
—migration assistance
programs, 45
—population groups, 45
—tribal colleges, 22
—tribal communities, 45
—unemployment rates, 46
Asian Americans/Pacific Islanders,
43–45
—employment patterns, 43, 44,
45
—geographic residence, 22, 44
—immigrants, 13, 44
—population groups, 43
—quotas, 44
—socioeconomic background,
44, 45
Assimilation, 13–14, 36–39
Bilingual education, 14, 42
Black Americans, 39–41
—census data, 40
—employment patterns, 40, 41,
43
—geographic residence, 22, 40
—immigrants, 13, 40

—income level, 40–41
Career mobility, 7
Census data, 36, 37, 40, 42, 43, 45
—American Indians/Alaskan
Natives, 45
—Asian Americans/Pacific
Islanders, 43
—Black Americans, 40
—Hispanic Americans, 42
Certification examinations, 24
Class mobility, 26
Colleges, 22
—historically Black, 22
—tribal, 22
Culture, 9–12
—background, xi, 7
—diversity, xi, xii, 13, 48
—justification, xii
—patterns, 12, 13
—socioeconomic, 12
—of teachers, teaching, 1–7
Degree attainment
—minority teachers, 18, 21–23
—parents, 27
—teachers, 18
Disadvantages
—economic, 10, 21, 27
—social, 10, 21
Discrimination, 14, 37, 39, 40, 42
Disincentives, 24, 34
Economical character, 1
Educational achievement, 11
—higher education, 18, 20–23,
29, 39
—K-12, 18, 20–22, 42
Educational attainment, 11, 17, 27, 39
—parent, 27

60